STANDARD GRADE | GENERAL | CREDIT

GAELIC (LEARNERS)
2007-2010

Fhuair am pròiseact seo taic bho Stòrlann Nàiseanta na Gàidhlig às leth Riaghaltas na h-Alba. Tha Stòrlann Nàiseanta na Gàidhlig a' faighinn taic bho Bhòrd n Gàidhlig.

Please note that some amendments have been made to the text in line with SQA's revised Gaelic Orthographic Conventions.

First exam published in 2007.
Published by Bright Red Publishing Ltd, 6 Stafford Street, Edinburgh EH3 7AU
tel: 0131 220 5804 fax: 0131 220 6710 info@brightredpublishing.co.uk www.brightredpublishing.co.uk

ISBN 978-1-84948-091-8

A CIP Catalogue record for this book is available from the British Library.

Bright Red Publishing is grateful to the copyright holders, as credited on the final page of the book, for permission to use their material. Every effort has been made to trace the copyright holders and to obtain their permission for the use of copyright material. Bright Red Publishing will be happy to receive information allowing us to rectify any error or omission in future editions.

STANDARD GRADE | GENERAL

2007

[BLANK PAGE]

FOR OFFICIAL USE

G

Total ☐

1240/408

NATIONAL	FRIDAY, 25 MAY	GAELIC (LEARNERS)
QUALIFICATIONS	2.00 PM – 2.45 PM	STANDARD GRADE
2007		General Level
		Reading

Fill in these boxes and read what is printed below.

Full name of centre

☐

Town

☐

Forename(s)

☐

Surname

☐

Date of birth
Day Month Year ☐☐☐☐☐☐

Scottish candidate number ☐☐☐☐☐☐☐

Number of seat ☐

Do not open this paper until you are told to do so.

When you are told to open the paper, read carefully the English introduction at the beginning, and then work through the paper, starting at Question 1.

When you think you know what to write for each item, write your answer **in English** in the space provided after the item. (You are not expected to fill all the spaces.)

Where boxes like this ☐ are provided, put a tick (✓) in the box beside the answer you think is correct.

You may use a Gaelic dictionary.

You must write any rough work in this paper.

Before leaving the examination room you must give this book to the invigilator. If you do not, you may lose all the marks for this paper.

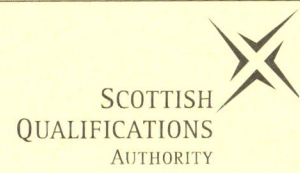
SCOTTISH
QUALIFICATIONS
AUTHORITY

©

Marks

Students write for the school magazine.

1. Calum writes about the Fèis.

> **Bha Fèis Òigridh ann am Bun-sgoil na Pàirce bho 7 gu 11 An Giblean. Bha clann a' bhaile a' gabhail pàirt. Bha seachdad aig an Fhèis.**
>
> **Seo na clasaichean a bha ann:**
> - **seinn**
> - **dràma**
> - **bogsa-ciùil**
> - **fidheall**
> - **a' phìob mhòr.**

(*a*) Where was the Fèis held?

_____

_____   2

(*b*) In which month did the Fèis take place?

_____   1

(*c*) How many children took part in the Fèis?

_____   1

(*d*) Name **four** of the classes offered at the Fèis.

    (i) _____

    (ii) _____

    (iii) _____

    (iv) _____   4

Marks

2. Alice writes about the Sports Centre.

> **Aig toiseach na seachdaine bha co-fharpais badmanton ann airson sgoilearan air a' chiad agus air an dàrna bliadhna. Ghabh ceud sgoilear pàirt anns a' cho-fharpais. Bha mòran chluicheadairean sgileil ann ach cha robh ann ach dà dhuais. Bhuannaich Anndra Caimbeul duais nan gillean agus Ealasaid NicDhòmhnaill duais nan nigheanan.**

(*a*) When did the badminton competition take place?

_____

_____   2

(*b*) (i) Which year groups were taking part?

_____

_____   2

(ii) How many students took part?

_____   1

(*c*) Who won

(i) the boys' competition?

_____

_____   2

(ii) the girls' competition?

_____

_____   2

DO NOT
WRITE IN
THIS
MARGIN

Marks

3. Victoria writes about the school dance.

> Bha dannsa na sgoile ann Dimàirt ron Nollaig. Chòrd e ris a h-uile duine.
>
> Thòisich an dannsa aig ochd uairean agus bha dà chòmhlan às an sgoil a' cluich. Chluich iad mòran de na h-òrain as fheàrr leam. Cha do sguir an dannsa gu aon uair deug.
>
> Bha ceapairean, suiteas, seòclaid agus cèicean ann.
>
> Bidh an ath dhannsa ann aig saor-làithean an t-samhraidh.

(a) When did the school dance take place?

_____

_____

_____   3

(b) Who was playing at the dance? Give a **detailed** answer.

_____

_____

_____   3

(c) At what time did the dance **finish**?

_____   1

(d) Name **three** things which they could get to eat.

(i) _____

(ii) _____

(iii) _____   3

(e) When is the next dance?

_____

_____   2

Marks

4. Sam writes about a sale of work.

> **Bidh fèill-reic ann an Talla a' Bhaile Disathairne 28 An t-Ògmhios airson airgead a chruinneachadh do dhaoine bochda ann an Afraga. Tha cluicheadair ball-coise ainmeil a' fosgladh na fèill-reic. Tha sinn an dòchas dà mhìle not a chruinneachadh.**
>
> **Thigibh ann tràth!**

(a) Where is the sale of work to be held?

_____

_____ **2**

(b) In what month is it to take place?

_____ **1**

(c) For whom is the money being raised?

_____

_____

_____ **3**

(d) Who will be opening the sale of work?

_____

_____

_____ **3**

(e) How much money do they hope to raise?

_____

_____ **2**

(f) What advice is given in the last sentence?

_____

_____ **2**

Marks

5. Students write some useful phrases.

(*a*)	**Chan eil mi a' tuigsinn**
(*b*)	**Chan eil fios agam**
(*c*)	**A bheil am pathadh ort?**
(*d*)	**Chan eil an t-acras orm**
(*e*)	**'S urrainn dhomh sgitheadh**
(*f*)	**A bheil thu trang?**
(*g*)	**Gabh mo leisgeul**
(*h*)	**Mòran taing**

Match the Gaelic phrases with the English phrases in the table below. Write the **correct letter** in the space provided.

1.   Are you busy?   ____

2.   Many thanks   ____

3.   I don't know   ____

4.   I can ski   ____

5.   I don't understand   ____

6.   Are you thirsty?   ____

7.   I am not hungry   ____

8.   Excuse me   ____

8

(50)

[*END OF QUESTION PAPER*]

G

1240/404

NATIONAL
QUALIFICATIONS
2007

FRIDAY, 25 MAY
9.45 AM – 10.15 AM

GAELIC (LEARNERS)
STANDARD GRADE
General Level
Listening Transcript

This paper must not be seen by any candidate.

The material overleaf is provided for use in an emergency only (eg the recording or equipment proving faulty) or where permission has been given in advance by SQA for the material to be read to candidates with additional support needs. The material must be read exactly as printed.

SCOTTISH
QUALIFICATIONS
AUTHORITY

Transcript–General Level

Carly, John and Kirsty are pupils at Invercarron High School. They are talking on their local radio station about their school trip last year.

Tha Carly, Iain agus Kirsty nan sgoilearan ann an Àrd-sgoil Inbhir Carrann. Tha iad ag innse air an stèisean rèidio aca mar a bha an turas-sgoile aca an-uiridh. Tha Anna gan cuideachadh.

John is the first to talk about the trip.

Question number one.

What does he say first of all?

Fàilte!

(30 seconds)

John continues.

Question number two.

(*a*) Where did they go on the school trip? Were they in England, or were they in Ireland, or were they in Wales? Tick the correct box.

Bha sinn ann an Èirinn.

(35 seconds)

(*b*) Which **two** types of transport did they use to get there?

Chaidh sinn ann air a' bhus agus air a' bhàt'-aiseig.

(30 seconds)

Question number three.

Name **three** of the things that John took with him to eat and drink on the journey.

Thug mi leam brisgein, seòclaid, suiteis agus uisge.

(30 seconds)

Ann, who was not on the trip, asks John a question.

Question number four.

(*a*)   What does she ask him?

Càit an robh sibh a' fuireach?

(*30 seconds*)

(*b*)   What does John reply?

Bha sinn a' fuireach ann an ostail-òigridh.

(*30 seconds*)

Carly says there were people from many different countries staying there.

(*c*)   Name the **three** countries she mentions.

Bha daoine ann às an Spàinn, às an Eadailt agus às an Òlaind.

(*30 seconds*)

Carly goes on to talk about some of the things they did.

Question number five.

(*a*)   Which of these **two** places did they visit? Tick **two** boxes.

Chaidh sinn gu caisteal agus gu eaglais.

(*30 seconds*)

(*b*)   What **three** activities did they do?

Bha sinn a' sreap, a' coiseachd agus a' seòladh.

(*30 seconds*)

(*c*)   What did Carly think of this? Give a **detailed** answer.

Chòrd e rium glè mhath.

(*30 seconds*)

[**Turn over**

Carly also says they visited a tourist centre which had a shop.

Question number six.

(a)   Which **three** things did Carly buy in this shop?

Cheannaich mi camara, leabhar agus dealbhan.

(30 seconds)

She also bought some presents in the shop.

(b)   For whom did she buy them?

Fhuair mi preusantan do mo phiuthar agus dom athair.

(30 seconds)

She paid for the presents in Euros.

(c)   How much did they cost altogether?

Chosg na preusantan fichead Euro uile-gu-lèir.

(30 seconds)

Kirsty now tells about a visit they made to the Irish-language television station, TG4.

Question number seven.

(a)   Which day did they go to TG4?

Chaidh sinn gu TG4 Diardaoin.

(30 seconds)

(b)   When did they arrive at TG4?

Ràinig sinn TG4 aig leth-uair an dèidh ceithir.

(30 seconds)

They saw a programme being broadcast live.

(c)   What kind of programme did they see? Was it a sports programme, or was it a cookery programme, or was it a news programme? Tick the correct box.

Chunnaic iad prògram naidheachdan.

(40 seconds)

Kirsty also talks about a trip they made to the Aran Islands.

Question number eight.

How long did the journey to the Aran Islands take?

Bha sinn uair a thìde air a' bhàta.

(30 seconds)

Ann asks Kirsty a question.

Question number nine.

(a)   What does she ask her?

Dè rinn sibh?

(30 seconds)

(b)   Where does Kirsty say they went? Give a **detailed** answer.

Chaidh sinn gu consairt ann an talla a' bhaile.

(30 seconds)

She gives more details.

(c)   What **three** things were the people doing?

Bha na daoine a' seinn, a' dannsa agus a' cluich na fidhle.

(30 seconds)

Kirsty sums up the trip.

Question number ten.

What is Kirsty's opinion of Ireland?

Tha Èirinn brèagha agus inntinneach.

(30 seconds)

End of test.

Now look over your answers.

[END OF TRANSCRIPT]

[BLANK PAGE]

FOR OFFICIAL USE

Total Mark

1240/403

| NATIONAL QUALIFICATIONS 2007 | FRIDAY, 25 MAY 9.45 AM – 10.15 AM | GAELIC (LEARNERS) STANDARD GRADE General Level Listening |

Fill in these boxes and read what is printed below.

Full name of centre

Town

Forename(s)

Surname

Date of birth
Day Month Year   Scottish candidate number   Number of seat

Do not open this paper until you are told to do so.

In this test, you have to listen carefully to a number of short passages in Gaelic to find the information asked for in the questions.

You will hear each passage three times, and then you will have time to write your answers. Answer **in English** in the spaces provided.

When you are told to open this paper, read the English introduction at the beginning. Follow the questions printed in the paper as you hear them, and then write your answers. Do not give up the first time you get stuck; leave a blank and keep trying.

As you listen to the passages, you may make notes, but only in this paper.

You are not allowed to leave the examination room until the end of the test.

Before leaving the examination room you must give this book to the invigilator. If you do not, you may lose all the marks for this paper.

SCOTTISH QUALIFICATIONS AUTHORITY

Marks

Carly, John and Kirsty are pupils at Invercarron High School. They are talking on their local radio station about their school trip last year.

John is the first to talk about the trip.

1. What does he say first of all?

_____   1

*   *   *   *   *

John continues.

2. (*a*)   Where did they go on the school trip? Were they in England, or were they in Ireland, or were they in Wales?

Tick (✓) the correct box.

	(✓)
England	
Ireland	
Wales	

1

(*b*)   Which **two** types of transport did they use to get there?

_____

_____   2

*   *   *   *   *

3. Name **three** of the things that John took with him to eat and drink on the journey.

_____

_____

_____   3

*   *   *   *   *

Marks

Ann, who was not on the trip, asks John a question.

4. (*a*)   What does she ask him?

_____

_____   **2**

(*b*)   What does John reply?

_____   **1**

Carly says there were people from many different countries staying there.

(*c*)   Name the **three** countries she mentions.

1   _____

2   _____

3   _____   **3**

*   *   *   *   *

[Turn over

Marks

Carly goes on to talk about some of the things they did.

5. (*a*)   Which of these **two** places did they visit?

Tick (✓) **two** boxes.

	(✓)
Sports centre	
Castle	
Church	
Cinema	
Shops	

2

(*b*)   What **three** activities did they do?

1 _____

2 _____

3 _____

3

(*c*)   What did Carly think of this? Give a **detailed** answer.

_____

_____

2

*   *   *   *   *

Marks

Carly also says they visited a tourist centre which had a shop.

6.　(*a*)　Which **three** things did Carly buy in this shop?

_____

_____

_____　　**3**

She also bought some presents in the shop.

(*b*)　For whom did she buy them?

_____

_____　　**2**

She paid for the presents in Euros.

(*c*)　How much did they cost altogether?

_____　　**1**

*　　*　　*　　*　　*

[Turn over

Marks

Kirsty now tells about a visit they made to the Irish-language television station, TG4.

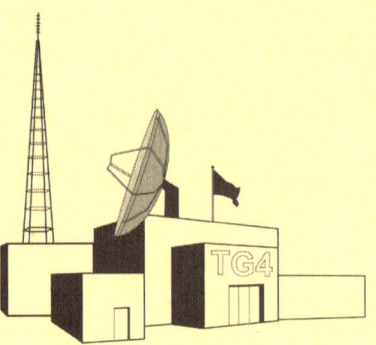

7. (*a*)   Which day did they go to TG4?

_____   1

(*b*)   When did they arrive at TG4?

_____

_____   2

They saw a programme being broadcast live.

(*c*)   What kind of programme did they see? Was it a sports programme, or was it a cookery programme, or was it a news programme?

Tick (✓) the correct box.

Sports   Cookery   News

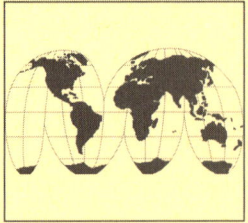

☐   ☐   ☐   1

*   *   *   *   *

Marks

Kirsty also talks about a trip they made to the Aran Islands.

8. How long did the journey to the Aran Islands take?

_____ 1

*   *   *   *   *

Ann asks Kirsty a question.

9. (*a*)   What does she ask her?

_____

_____ 2

(*b*)   Where does Kirsty say they went?

Give a **detailed** answer.

_____

_____ 2

She gives more details.

(*c*)   What **three** things were the people doing?

1 _____

2 _____

3 _____ 3

*   *   *   *   *

[Turn over for Question 10 on *Page eight*

Marks

Kirsty sums up the trip.

10. What is Kirsty's opinion of Ireland?

_____   **2**

*   *   *   *   *

Total marks (40)

[*END OF QUESTION PAPER*]

2007

[BLANK PAGE]

FOR OFFICIAL USE

C

Total

1240/409

NATIONAL
QUALIFICATIONS
2007

FRIDAY, 25 MAY
3.00 PM – 3.45 PM

GAELIC (LEARNERS)
STANDARD GRADE
Credit Level
Reading

Fill in these boxes and read what is printed below.

Full name of centre

Town

Forename(s)

Surname

Date of birth
Day Month Year

Scottish candidate number

Number of seat

Do not open this paper until you are told to do so.

When you are told to open the paper, read carefully the English introduction at the beginning, and then work through the paper, starting at Question 1.

When you think you know what to write for each item, write your answer **in English** in the space provided after the item. (You are not expected to fill all the spaces.)

You may use a Gaelic dictionary.

You must write any rough work in this paper.

Before leaving the examination room you must give this book to the invigilator. If you do not, you may lose all the marks for this paper.

SCOTTISH
QUALIFICATIONS
AUTHORITY

©

Marks

Students write for the school magazine.

1. Calum writes about a novel he has read.

> **Leugh mi an leabhar *Turas air Bàta Thormoid* ann am mìos. Is toigh leam a bhith a' leughadh a h–uile oidhche. Bidh mi a' faighinn leabhraichean às an leabharlann.**
>
> **Bha còignear anns an sgeulachd seo, triùir bhalach agus dithis nighean. Is e Anndra aon de na prìomh charactaran anns an nobhail. Thug athair Anndra iad gu eilean air bàta.**
>
> **Dh'fhuirich iad air an eilean airson cola-deug. B' e an samhradh a bha ann agus bha an t-sìde blàth agus tioram.**

(a) How long did it take Calum to read the novel?

_____   1

(b) How often does Calum read?

_____

_____   2

(c) How many characters are there in the story?

_____   1

(d) Who was Andrew?

_____

_____

_____   3

Marks

1. **(continued)**

(*e*)   Where did they go **and** who took them there?

_____

_____   2

(*f*)   How long were they away?

_____   1

(*g*)   (i) What time of year was it?

_____   1

(ii) What was the weather like?

_____

_____   2

[Turn over

Marks

2. Calum continues to write about the novel.

> **Tha na balaich agus na nigheanan a' fuireach ann am baile beag air taobh an iar Alba. Tha iad uile eadar trì bliadhna deug agus sia bliadhna deug a dh'aois. Is e caraidean Anndra a th' annta.**
>
> **Chaidh iad gu eilean creagach, bòidheach. Tha an nobhail ag innse mu na cur-seachadan aca: sreap, seòladh, snàmh, iasgach agus coiseachd.**
>
> **Chòrd an nobhail rium. Bha i èibhinn.**

(*a*) Where **exactly** do the boys and girls live?

  4

(*b*) How old are they?

  3

(*c*) Mention **two** ways in which Calum describes the island.

(i) _____

(ii) _____   2

Marks

2. **(continued)**

   (*d*)   Name **four** of their pastimes on the island.

   (i) _____

   (ii) _____

   (iii) _____

   (iv) _____   4

   (*e*)   Why did he enjoy the novel?

   _____   1

   [Turn over

Marks

3. Finlay writes about a concert.

An dàrna Disathairne anns a' Chèitean, chaidh mi gu consairt ann an Sruighlea. B' e consairt do dh'òigridh a bha ann. Bha e eadar-dhealaichte bho chonsairtean eile oir chaidh an consairt a chumail air taobh a-muigh a' chaisteil.

Thòisich an consairt tràth feasgar agus bha e a' dol gu anmoch. Bha mu chòig mìle deug neach aig a' chonsairt agus abair gun robh oidhche sgoinneil aig a h-uile duine. A bharrachd air còmhlain à Alba, bha còmhlan à Èirinn ann cuideachd. Bha an còmhlan à Èirinn beòthail. Chòrd na còmhlain uile rinn. Bha na goireasan aig a'chonsairt math dha-rìribh. Bha e uabhasach cudromach nach robh an t-uisge ann agus nach robh i fuar.

(*a*) When did Finlay go the concert? Give a **detailed** answer.

_____

_____

_____   3

(*b*) The concert was held in Stirling. Where exactly?

_____

_____   2

(*c*) When did the concert start?

_____

_____   2

(*d*) What is said about the band from Ireland?

_____   1

DO NOT WRITE IN THIS MARGIN

Marks

3. (continued)

(*e*) What was the weather like? Give a **detailed** answer.

____

____

____ **3**

[Turn over

Marks

4. James writes about working on a farm.

> **Bha tuathanas faisg air taigh mo sheanar agus dh'iarr mi obair air Seòras, an tuathanach. Fhuair mi an cothrom sin. Bha mi glè thoilichte oir bha mi ag iarraidh eòlas obrach fhaighinn agus is toigh leam beathaichean.**
>
> **Tha mi a' smaoineachadh gu bheil an obair cruaidh ach inntinneach. A h-uile madainn bidh Seòras ag èirigh aig leth-uair an dèidh còig. Tha na h-uairean aige fada.**

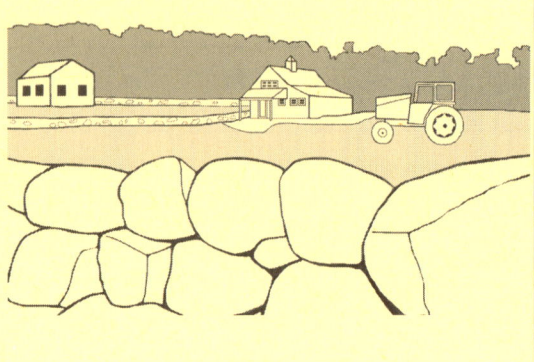

(*a*) Where is the farm?

_____

_____

_____   3

(*b*) How did James get the opportunity to work on the farm?

_____

_____   2

(*c*) Why was he pleased about this opportunity? Give **two** reasons.

(i) _____

_____

(ii) _____

_____   4

(*d*) What does he think of the work?

_____

_____   2

DO NOT WRITE IN THIS MARGIN

Marks

4. (continued)

(*e*) What does he say about George's working day?

5

[Turn over for Question 5 on *Page ten*

Marks

5.   Gary writes about his pet dog, Dìleas.

> Is fìor thoigh leam an cù agam, Dìleas.
> Fhuair mi e nuair a bha e ceithir mìosan
> a dh'aois bho mo phàrantan airson mo
> cho-là-breith. Tha dath dubh agus geal
> air. Is e cù toilichte, càirdeil a tha ann.
> Bidh e a'dol a-mach còmhla riumsa
> agus bidh mòran spòrs againn.
> Feumaidh mi a ràdh gu bheil eagal aige
> bhon chat agam.
>
> Bidh e a' coiseachd còmhla rium don sgoil agus an uair sin tillidh
> e dhachaigh leis fhèin. Aig leth-uair an dèidh trì, nuair a
> chluinneas e clag na sgoile, bidh e a' comhartaich ag iarraidh
> a-mach agus ruithidh e don sgoil gam choinneachadh. Chan eil
> rud sam bith ann cho prìseil dhomh ris a' chù agam. Uill, mo
> phàrantan – is dòcha!

According to the passage above, which of the following statements are true?
Put a tick (✓) where the statement is true. Choose **six** statements.

TRUE

Dìleas . . .

was 4 months when Gary got him. ☐

is not a friendly dog. ☐

is brown. ☐

likes sausages. ☐

is a happy dog. ☐

will go out with anyone. ☐

is frightened of Gary's cat. ☐

walks with Gary to school. ☐

barks when he hears the school bell. ☐

runs to the school to meet him. ☐

waits patiently for him at home. ☐

6

(60)

[*END OF QUESTION PAPER*]

1240/406

NATIONAL QUALIFICATIONS 2007	FRIDAY, 25 MAY 10.30 AM – 11.00 AM	GAELIC (LEARNERS) STANDARD GRADE Credit Level Listening Transcript

This paper must not be seen by any candidate.

The material overleaf is provided for use in an emergency only (eg the recording or equipment proving faulty) or where permission has been given in advance by SQA for the material to be read to candidates with additional support needs. The material must be read exactly as printed.

SCOTTISH
QUALIFICATIONS
AUTHORITY

Transcript – Credit Level

Instructions to reader:

For each item, read the English **once**, and then read the Gaelic **three** times with an interval of seven seconds between the readings. On completion of the third reading, pause for the length of time indicated in brackets after each item, to allow the candidates to write their answers.

Carly, Kirsty, John and Ann are making a series of programmes at their radio station.

Tha Carly, Kirsty, Iain agus Anna air a bhith a' dèanamh sreath phrògraman aig an stèisean rèidio aca.

Kirsty is the first at the microphone.

Question number one.

What does Kirsty say to the listeners?

Ciamar a tha sibh an-diugh?

(*30 seconds*)

She tells us about Poolfearn, the village they live in.

Question number two.

(*a*)   Where is the village?

Tha am baile againn ann an taobh tuath na h-Alba.

(*30 seconds*)

(*b*)   What further details does she give about its location?

Tha e caogad mìle a-mach à Inbhir Nis.

(*30 seconds*)

She says more about Poolfearn.

Question number three.

(*a*)   What is Poolfearn like?

'S e baile beag càirdeil a tha ann am Poll Feàrna.

(*35 seconds*)

(*b*)   How many people live there?

Tha mu thrì cheud neach a' fuireach ann.

(*35 seconds*)

Kirsty goes on to talk about the facilities in Poolfearn.

Question number four.

(a)   Name **three** of the facilities in the village.

Tha oifis a' phuist, bun-sgoil, amar-snàmh agus ionad-fiosrachaidh ann.

(40 seconds)

(b)   **When** did one of these facilities open?

Dh'fhosgail an t-amar-snàmh an-uiridh.

(30 seconds)

(c)   How much did it cost?

Chosg e còig ceud mìle not.

(30 seconds)

Carly takes over from Kirsty. She tells about the hotel in Poolfearn.

Question number five.

(a)   Where, **exactly**, is the hotel?

Tha an taigh-òsta faisg air meadhan a' bhaile.

(40 seconds)

(b)   How many people work there?

Tha ochdnar ag obair anns an taigh-òsta.

(40 seconds)

She goes on to talk about the people who own the hotel.

Question number six.

(a)   What are the names of the owners?

'S ann le Mairead agus Coinneach MacLeòid a tha e.

(30 seconds)

(b)   What family do they have?

Tha balach agus nighean aca.

(40 seconds)

[Turn over

Carly sometimes works in the hotel.

Question number seven.

(a)   What exactly does she do in the hotel kitchen?

Tha mi ag obair anns a' chidsin, a' nighe nan soithichean agus a' glanadh an làir.

(35 seconds)

(b)   How does she feel about her work, **and** why?

Cha toigh leam an obair idir oir tha e sgìtheil.

(35 seconds)

John is next to speak. He only moved to Poolfearn a few months ago.

Question number eight.

(a)   What is John's address?

Tha mi a' fuireach aig seachd Rathad na Beinne.

(35 seconds)

(b)   Name **three** of the rooms he mentions in his house.

Tha rùm-suidhe, rùm-ithe, rùm-teaghlaich agus rùm-ionnlaid anns an taigh agam. 'S e taigh mòr spaideil a th' ann.

(35 seconds)

John has a notice on the door of his bedroom.

Question number nine.

What does it say?

Cunnart! Na tig a-steach!

(35 seconds)

He has one complaint about Poolfearn – the weather!

Question number ten.

Why doesn't he like it?

Tha e cho fliuch agus cho garbh anns a' gheamhradh.

(40 seconds)

Ann is the last of the four to speak. She has news of a competition that the village entered for.

Question number eleven.

(*a*)   What is the title of the competition?

'S e "An t-Àite as Fheàrr" ainm na farpaise.

(*30 seconds*)

(*b*)   Where was Poolfearn placed in the competition?

Fhuair am baile againn an dàrna duais.

(*30 seconds*)

Ann, Carly, Kirsty and John have come to the end of their programme-making. Just before they go, Ann tells listeners how they can get more information about Poolfearn.

Question number twelve.

Where can listeners get more information?

Gheibh sibh barrachd fiosrachaidh air an làrach-lìn againn.

(*35 seconds*)

End of test.

Now look over your answers.

[*END OF TRANSCRIPT*]

[BLANK PAGE]

FOR OFFICIAL USE

C

Total Mark

1240/405

| NATIONAL QUALIFICATIONS 2007 | FRIDAY, 25 MAY 10.30 AM – 11.00 AM | **GAELIC (LEARNERS) STANDARD GRADE** Credit Level Listening |

Fill in these boxes and read what is printed below.

Full name of school or college

Town

Forename(s)

Surname

Date of birth
Day Month Year

Scottish candidate number

Number of seat

Do not open this paper until you are told to do so.

In this test, you have to listen carefully to a number of short passages in Gaelic to find the information asked for in the questions.

You will hear each passage three times, and then you will have time to write your answers. Answer **in English** in the spaces provided.

When you are told to open this paper, read the English introduction at the beginning. Follow the questions printed in the paper as you hear them, and then write your answers. Do not give up the first time you get stuck; leave a blank and keep trying.

As you listen to the passages, you may make notes, but only in this paper.

You are not allowed to leave the examination room until the end of the test.

Before leaving the examination room you must give this book to the invigilator. If you do not, you may lose all the marks for this paper.

SCOTTISH QUALIFICATIONS AUTHORITY

©

Marks

Carly, Kirsty, John and Ann are making a series of programmes at their radio station.

Kirsty is the first at the microphone.

1. What does Kirsty say to the listeners?

_____

_____   1

*　*　*　*　*

She tells us about Poolfearn, the village they live in.

2. (a) Where is the village?

_____

_____   2

(b) What further details does she give about its location?

_____

_____

_____

_____   4

*　*　*　*　*

She says more about Poolfearn.

3. (a) What is Poolfearn like?

_____

_____   2

(b) How many people live there?

_____

_____   2

*　*　*　*　*

Marks

Kirsty goes on to talk about the facilities in Poolfearn.

4. (*a*) Name **three** of the facilities in the village.

1 _____

2 _____

3 _____   **3**

(*b*) **When** did one of these facilities open?

_____   **1**

(*c*) How much did it cost?

_____

_____   **2**

*   *   *   *   *

Carly takes over from Kirsty. She tells about the hotel in Poolfearn.

5. (*a*) Where, **exactly**, is the hotel?

_____

_____

_____   **3**

(*b*) How many people work there?

_____   **1**

*   *   *   *   *

[Turn over

Marks

She goes on to talk about the people who own the hotel.

6. (*a*) What are the names of the owners?

_____

_____

_____   **3**

(*b*) What family do they have?

_____

_____   **2**

*   *   *   *   *

Carly sometimes works in the hotel.

7. (*a*) What exactly does she do in the hotel kitchen?

_____

_____

_____

_____   **4**

(*b*) How does she feel about her work, **and** why?

_____

_____

_____   **3**

*   *   *   *   *

Marks

John is next to speak. He only moved to Poolfearn a few months ago.

8. (*a*)   What is John's address?

_____

_____

_____   3

(*b*)   Name **three** of the rooms he mentions in his house.

1 _____

2 _____

3 _____   3

*   *   *   *   *

John has a notice on the door of his bedroom.

9.   What does it say?

_____

_____

_____   3

*   *   *   *   *

He has one complaint about Poolfearn—the weather!

10.   Why doesn't he like it?

_____

_____

_____

_____   4

*   *   *   *   *

[Turn over for Questions 11 and 12 on *Page six*

Marks

Ann is the last of the four to speak. She has news of a competition that the village entered for.

11. (*a*) What is the title of the competition?

_____

_____   **2**

(*b*) Where was Poolfearn placed in the competition?

_____   **1**

*   *   *   *   *

Ann, Carly, Kirsty and John have come to the end of their programme-making. Just before they go, Ann tells listeners how they can get more information about Poolfearn.

12. Where can listeners get more information?

_____   **1**

*   *   *   *   *

Total marks (50)

[END OF QUESTION PAPER]

STANDARD GRADE | GENERAL | CREDIT

2007

[BLANK PAGE]

1241/410

| NATIONAL QUALIFICATIONS 2007 | FRIDAY, 25 MAY 11.15 AM – 12.15 PM | **GAELIC (LEARNERS)** **STANDARD GRADE** General/Credit Level (Optional) Writing |

Do not turn over this paper until you are told to do so.

You may use a Gaelic dictionary.

Write your answers in the booklet provided.

SCOTTISH QUALIFICATIONS AUTHORITY

Answer, in Gaelic, <u>two</u> questions. **One** question must be answered from Section A, and **one** question from Section B. Your answer to Section A should be brief but answer the question, while for Section B more detail is required. To help you write, you have been given checklists, graphics and a suggested way to start each piece.

SECTION A

EITHER

1. You are away on your holidays, and are writing a postcard to a friend at home.

   In your card, you may include:

   - where you are on your holidays

   - what your accommodation is like

   - what you've been doing

   - what the weather is like

   - whether you're enjoying it

   - any other relevant information.

Paris, 23 An t-Iuchar, 2007. **Hai, a Mhàiri,** **Tha mi ann am Paris an-dràsta . . .** 	**Màiri Ghrannd,** **3 Rathad a' Chaisteil,** **Inbhir Carrann,** **Alba.**

OR

2. Your local tourist board is asking for information about a concert by *Celt Rock*. They have asked you to design a hand-out for a concert with the band. **Remember to write in sentences.**

On the hand-out, you may wish to give details of:

- when the concert is on
- where it is being held
- when it starts and finishes
- how much it costs
- what will be on sale
- any other relevant information.

Celt Rock

Tha Consairt le Celt Rock ann an talla Inbhir Carrann . . .

[Turn over for Section B on *Page four*

SECTION B

EITHER

1. You have been asked to write an article for a website for teenagers about a holiday you enjoyed.

    You may include in your article:

    *   where you went

    *   how you got there, and how long it took

    *   who you went with

    *   where you stayed

    *   what you did

    *   where you went – tourist attractions, shops, concerts, and so on

    *   what souvenirs/presents you bought

    *   how much they cost

    *   what the weather was like

    *   why you enjoyed it

    *   any other relevant information.

ÒIGRIDH

Saor-làithean anns an Fhraing

le Catrìona NicRath

Chaidh sinn . . . an-uiridh, agus bha mi a' fuireach ann an taigh-òsta . . .

OR

2. You have just been at a concert with the rock band *Celt Rock*. You are writing a letter to a friend, telling them about the concert.

In your letter, you may include:

- where the concert took place
- who you went with
- when the concert started
- how much it cost to get in
- how many band members there were
- what the band members looked like
- which instruments the band members played
- which numbers they played
- when the concert finished
- whether you enjoyed it, and why
- any other relevant information.

Give the letter a correct beginning and ending.

          17 Rathad na h-Eaglaise
          An Gearastan.
          3 An Lùnastal, 2007

Anna Chòir,

Bha mi aig consairt le Celt Rock ann an Inbhir Carrann . . .

Sgrìobh air ais a dh'aithghearr.
    Le dùrachd,
        Dòmhnall
             x

[END OF QUESTION PAPER]

[BLANK PAGE]

2008

[BLANK PAGE]

FOR OFFICIAL USE

G

Total

1240/408

NATIONAL
QUALIFICATIONS
2008

WEDNESDAY, 28 MAY
2.00 PM – 2.45 PM

GAELIC (LEARNERS)
STANDARD GRADE
General Level
Reading

Fill in these boxes and read what is printed below.

Full name of centre

Town

Forename(s)

Surname

Date of birth

Day   Month   Year   Scottish candidate number   Number of seat

Do not open this paper until you are told to do so.

When you are told to open the paper, read carefully the English introduction at the beginning, and then work through the paper, starting at Question 1.

When you think you know what to write for each item, write your answer **in English** in the space provided after the item. (You are not expected to fill all the spaces.)

Where boxes like this ☐ are provided, put a tick (✓) in the box beside the answer you think is correct.

You may use a Gaelic dictionary.

You must write any rough work in this paper.

Before leaving the examination room you must give this book to the invigilator. If you do not, you may lose all the marks for this paper.

©

Marks

A group of fourth-year pupils write about their favourite activities.

1.   Iain writes about his favourite activity.

> Is toigh leam iasgach. Thòisich mi ag iasgach nuair a bha mi sia bliadhna a dh'aois. Bidh mi a' dol a-mach a dh'iasgach air bàta còmhla ri mo sheanair. 'S e bàta mòr, dearg a th' aige. Is toigh leam a bhith ag iasgach aig muir agus air loch. Bidh mo bhràthair beag a' tighinn còmhla rinn uaireannan.

(a)   How old was Iain when he started fishing?

_____   1

(b)   Who does he go fishing with?

_____   1

(c)   What does the boat look like?

_____

_____   2

(d)   Where does Iain like to fish?

_____

_____   2

Marks

2.   Caroline tells what she does.

> **Bidh mi ag obair air tuathanas. Tha crodh agus caoraich againn agus tha m' athair uabhasach trang. Bidh mo mhàthair a' cuideachadh aig na saor-làithean.**
>
> **Is fheàrr leam a bhith a' fuireach air an dùthaich oir tha i nas brèagha nam baile mòr.**

(a)   Where does Caroline work?

_____   1

(b)   What kind of animals do they have?

_____

_____   2

(c)   What does she write about her father? Give a **detailed** answer.

_____

_____   2

(d)   What does she write about her mother? Give a **detailed** answer.

_____

_____   2

(e)   Why does she prefer living in the countryside?

_____

_____   2

[Turn over

DO NOT
WRITE IN
THIS
MARGIN

Marks

3. Christopher writes about his favourite hobby.

> **Tha seòladh a' còrdadh rium. Thòisich mi a' seòladh o chionn bliadhna. Bha mi a' seòladh anns an t-samhradh còmhla ri Anndra, mo cho-ogha. Is toigh leam a bhith a' seòladh nuair a tha gaoth ann. Bu toigh leam bàta ùr, luath fhaighinn aon latha.**

(*a*)   What is Christopher's opinion of sailing?

_____   1

(*b*)   When did he start sailing?

_____

_____   2

(*c*)   Who is Anndra?

_____   2

(*d*)   What kind of weather does he like sailing in?

_____   1

(*e*)   What kind of boat would Christopher like to have one day?

_____

_____   2

Marks

4.   Anna writes about the activity she prefers.

> 'S fheàrr leamsa marcachd. Chan eil each agam ach bidh mi a' dol gu stàball faisg air an taigh againn. Is toigh leam an t-each. Tha e àrd agus donn agus tha a nàdar còir. Tha marcachd a' cosg ochd notaichean airson uair a thìde. Is e cur-seachad daor a th' ann ach tha e sgoinneil.

(a)   What does Anna enjoy doing?

_____   1

(b)   Where does she go to do this?

_____

_____

_____   3

(c)   Describe the animal **in detail**.

_____

_____

_____

_____   4

(d)   In the last sentence, what does she say about this hobby?

_____

_____   2

[Turn over

Marks

5. Amanda writes about her favourite pastime, photography.

> 'S e togail dhealbhan an cur-seachad agam. Thòisich mi aig àm na Nollaige an-uiridh. Tha dà chamara agam. Fhuair mi camara didseatach bho mo bhràthair mòr. Is toigh leam a bhith a' togail dhealbhan de mo theaghlach. Tha e furasta a bhith a' togail dhealbhan de mo phiuthar as òige oir tha i cho laghach agus cho èibhinn. Tha mi an dòchas na dealbhan agam fhaicinn ann an iris ainmeil aon latha.

(*a*) When did Amanda start taking photographs?

_____

_____   2

(*b*) Who did she get a digital camera from?

_____

_____   2

(*c*) (i) Who does she say is easy to photograph?

_____

_____   2

    (ii) Why is this?

_____

_____   2

(*d*) Where does she hope to see her photographs one day?

_____

_____   2

Marks

6. Here are some reasons the pupils gave for having hobbies. Match the Gaelic with the English. One has been done for you.

1.	**Tha e math dhut.**	*a)*	I make new friends.
2.	**Tha e inntinneach.**	*b)*	I have lots of fun.
3.	**Bidh mi ag ionnsachadh.**	*c)*	I like exercise.
4.	**Tha mòran spòrs agam.**	*d)*	It is interesting.
5.	**'S toigh leam eacarsaich.**	*e)*	I keep healthy.
6.	**Is toigh leam a bhith a-muigh.**	*f)*	It is good for you.
7.	**Bidh mi a' cumail fallain.**	*g)*	I like being outside.
8.	**Bidh mi a' dèanamh caraidean ùra.**	*h)*	I am learning.

1.   **f**
2.   _____
3.   _____
4.   _____
5.   _____
6.   _____
7.   _____
8.   _____

7

(50)

[END OF QUESTION PAPER]

[BLANK PAGE]

G

1240/404

NATIONAL
QUALIFICATIONS
2008

WEDNESDAY, 28 MAY
9.45 AM – 10.15 AM

GAELIC (LEARNERS)
STANDARD GRADE
General Level
Listening Transcript

This paper must not be seen by any candidate.

The material overleaf is provided for use in an emergency only (eg the recording or equipment proving faulty) or where permission has been given in advance by SQA for the material to be read to candidates with additional support needs. The material must be read exactly as printed.

Transcript – General Level

The Gaelic class in Penifern High School is making a CD for a school in Canada. They are telling about themselves.

Tha an clas Gàidhlig ann an Àrd-sgoil Pheighinn Fheàrna a' dèanamh CD airson sgoil ann an Canada. Tha iad ag innse mun deidhinn fhèin.

Calum is the first to speak. He recently took part in an athletics competition.

Question number one.

Where was the competition held?

Bha mi ann an Glaschu.

(*20 seconds*)

Question number two.

(*a*)   What was the first day of the competition?

'S e Diardaoin a' chiad latha den fharpais.

(*20 seconds*)

(*b*)   At what time did it start on the first day?

Thòisich i aig leth-uair an dèidh naoi.

(*30 seconds*)

(*c*)   What day did the competition finish?

Chrìochnaich an fharpais Disathairne.

(*20 seconds*)

Question number three.

Where was Calum staying while he was taking part in the competition? Give a **detailed** answer.

Bha mi a' fuireach ann an taigh-òsta faisg air an ionad-spòrs.

(*40 seconds*)

Question number four.

What prize did he get in one of his competitions?

Fhuair mi an dàrna duais.

(*30 seconds*)

It's Catriona's turn to talk. She has just been doing work experience in a primary school.

Question number five.

(a) How old were the pupils she was working with?

Bha a' chlann seachd agus ochd bliadhna a dh'aois.

(*30 seconds*)

She was helping them with their schoolwork.

(b) Name **three** of the activities she was helping them with.

Bha mi a' cuideachadh le sgrìobhadh, leughadh, peantadh agus còcaireachd.

(*40 seconds*)

(c) What was the name of the teacher whose class she was with?

Bha mi ag obair còmhla ri Seònaid NicAonghais, tidsear a' chlas.

(*30 seconds*)

Donna then talks about a concert she was at.

Question number six.

(a) How much did the concert cost?

Chosg e deich notaichean agus caogad sgillinn.

(*30 seconds*)

(b) How many were in the band? Was it three, or was it four, or was it five? Tick the correct box.

Bha ceathrar anns a' chòmhlan.

(*20 seconds*)

(c) What month was the concert held in?

Bha e anns an Lùnastal.

(*20 seconds*)

[**Turn over**

The concert was in Aberdeen, a long way from Penifern.

Question number seven.

(*a*)   How did Donna get there?

Chaidh mi ann air an trèana agus air a' bhus.

(*30 seconds*)

(*b*)   How long did it take her to get there?

Thug mi ceithir uairean a thìde a' dol ann.

(*30 seconds*)

(*c*)   Who went to the concert with her?

Chaidh mi ann còmhla ri caraidean.

(*20 seconds*)

Donna tells about the band's singer.

Question number eight.

(*a*)   What do we find out about her?

(*b*)   What does the singer want to do?

'S toigh leatha Alba agus tha i ag iarraidh fuireach anns an Eilean Sgitheanach.

(*40 seconds*)

Question number nine.

Which **three** instruments did they play? Tick the **three** correct boxes.

Bha iad a' cluich giotàr, drumaichean agus meur-chlàr.

(*40 seconds*)

Question number ten.

Where was the band from?

Bha an còmhlan à Èirinn a Tuath.

(*30 seconds*)

After the concert, Donna says that she went for something to eat.

Question number eleven.

What **two** things did she have?

Ghabh mi iasg agus sliseagan.

(*30 seconds*)

Calum makes some final comments.

Question number twelve.

Where are they going?

Tha sinn a' dol gu club-òigridh a' bhaile a-nis.

(*30 seconds*)

Question number thirteen.

What is his final comment?

Beannachd leibh an-dràsta.

(*30 seconds*)

End of test.

Now look over your answers.

[END OF TRANSCRIPT]

[BLANK PAGE]

FOR OFFICIAL USE

Total Mark

1240/403

NATIONAL
QUALIFICATIONS
2008

WEDNESDAY, 28 MAY
9.45 AM – 10.15 AM

GAELIC (LEARNERS)
STANDARD GRADE
General Level
Listening

Fill in these boxes and read what is printed below.

Full name of centre

Town

Forename(s)

Surname

Date of birth
Day Month Year   Scottish candidate number   Number of seat

Do not open this paper until you are told to do so.

In this test, you have to listen carefully to a number of short passages in Gaelic to find the information asked for in the questions.

You will hear each passage three times, and then you will have time to write your answers. Answer **in English** in the spaces provided.

When you are told to open this paper, read the English introduction at the beginning. Follow the questions printed in the paper as you hear them, and then write your answers. Do not give up the first time you get stuck; leave a blank and keep trying.

As you listen to the passages, you may make notes, but only in this paper.

You are not allowed to leave the examination room until the end of the test.

Before leaving the examination room you must give this book to the invigilator. If you do not, you may lose all the marks for this paper.

DO NOT
WRITE IN
THIS
MARGIN

The Gaelic class in Penifern High School is making a CD for a school in Canada. *Marks*
They are telling about themselves.

Calum is the first to speak. He recently took part in an athletics competition.

1. Where was the competition held?

_____   1

*   *   *   *   *

2. (*a*)   What was the first day of the competition?

_____   1

(*b*)   At what time did it start on the first day?

_____

_____   2

(*c*)   What day did the competition finish?

_____   1

*   *   *   *   *

3. Where was Calum staying while he was taking part in the competition?
    Give a **detailed** answer.

_____

_____

_____   3

*   *   *   *   *

4. What prize did he get in one of his competitions?

_____   1

*   *   *   *   *

Marks

It's Catriona's turn to talk. She has just been doing work experience in a primary school.

5. (*a*) How old were the pupils she was working with?

_____

_____ 2

She was helping them with their schoolwork.

(*b*) Name **three** of the activities she was helping them with.

1 _____

2 _____

3 _____ 3

(*c*) What was the name of the teacher whose class she was with?

_____

_____ 2

* * * * *

[Turn over

Marks

Donna then talks about a concert she was at.

6. (*a*) How much did the concert cost?

_____ **2**

(*b*) How many were in the band? Was it three, or was it four, or was it five?
Tick (✓) the correct box.

	(✓)
Three	
Four	
Five	

1

(*c*) What month was the concert held in?

_____ **1**

*   *   *   *   *

The concert was in Aberdeen, a long way from Penifern.

7. (*a*) How did Donna get there?

_____

_____ **2**

(*b*) How long did it take her to get there?

_____

_____ **2**

(*c*) Who went to the concert with her?

_____ **1**

*   *   *   *   *

Donna tells about the band's singer.

8. (*a*) What do we find out about her?

_____

_____   2

(*b*) What does the singer want to do?

_____

_____   2

*   *   *   *   *

9. Which **three** instruments did they play?

Tick (✓) the **three** correct boxes.

3

*   *   *   *   *

10. Where was the band from?

_____

_____   2

*   *   *   *   *

[Turn over for Questions 11, 12 and 13 on *Page six*

Marks

DO NOT WRITE IN THIS MARGIN

Marks

After the concert, Donna says that she went for something to eat.

11. What **two** things did she have?

_____

_____   2

*   *   *   *   *

Calum makes some final comments.

12. Where are they going?

_____

_____   2

*   *   *   *   *

13. What is his final comment?

_____

_____   2

*   *   *   *   *

Total marks (40)

[END OF QUESTION PAPER]

2008

[BLANK PAGE]

FOR OFFICIAL USE

C

Total ☐

1240/409

NATIONAL
QUALIFICATIONS
2008

WEDNESDAY, 28 MAY
3.00 PM – 3.45 PM

**GAELIC (LEARNERS)
STANDARD GRADE**
Credit Level
Reading

Fill in these boxes and read what is printed below.

Full name of centre

☐

Town

☐

Forename(s)

☐

Surname

☐

Date of birth
Day Month Year   Scottish candidate number   Number of seat

☐ ☐ ☐   ☐ ☐ ☐ ☐ ☐   ☐

Do not open this paper until you are told to do so.

When you think you know what to write for each item, write your answer **in English** in the space provided after the item. (You are not expected to fill all the spaces.)

You may use a Gaelic dictionary.

You must write any rough work in this paper.

Before leaving the examination room you must give this book to the invigilator. If you do not, you may lose all the marks for this paper.

[Blank Page]

Marks

1. A group of fourth-year pupils visit their local leisure centre. Catriona reads from the notice board.

Fèis Spòrs

- **Spòrs is fealla-dhà gu leòr**
- **A' tòiseachadh aig an deireadh-sheachdain**
- **Airson sgoilearan anns an àrd-sgoil**
- **Faodaidh sibh pàirt a ghabhail ann am farpaisean**

Ma tha ùidh agaibh san Fhèis, tha Latha Fosgailte gu bhith ann Disathairne, 20 An Lùnastal.

(a) When are the sporting activities starting?

_____   1

(b) For whom are the activities intended?

_____

_____   2

(c) What can you take part in?

_____   1

(d) When is the Open Day to be held?

_____

_____   2

[Turn over

Marks

2. Catriona goes to the leisure centre on Saturday. She is given a leaflet and reads the following.

Ball-coise 	**Tha sinn ag iarraidh mu fhichead cluicheadair airson sgioba ball-coise a dhèanamh suas a chluicheas an aghaidh sgiobaidhean eile ann an Alba. Gheibh an sgioba a bhuannaicheas Cupa na Fèis.**
Iomain 	**Tha iomain air a bhith soirbheachail aig an ionad-spòrs againn airson iomadh bliadhna. Tha sinn ag iarraidh sgioba comasach. Feumaidh sibh a bhith deònach siubhal.**
Snàmh 	**Aig àm na Nollaige, tha co-fharpais shònraichte gu bhith ann am Pàislig. Tha a' cho-fharpais fosgailte do shnàmhadair sam bith a bhuannaich ann am farpaisean ionadail.**
Ruith 	**Bidh buidheann a' dol a-mach a ruith dà uair san t-seachdain. Tha sinn an dòchas rèisean a chur air dòigh anns an Earrach airson nan ruitheadairean a tha ag iarraidh a dhol gu farpaisean nàiseanta.**

(*a*) (i) How many players do they want for the football?

_____

_____ 2

(ii) Who will the team be playing against?

_____

_____

_____ 3

(*b*) (i) What is said about shinty at the sports centre?

_____ 1

(ii) What must those taking part in shinty be willing to do?

_____ 1

Marks

2. **(continued)**

(*c*) Who is eligible to swim at the event to be held in Paisley?

_____

_____

_____   3

(*d*)   (i) At what time of year are the running events?

_____   1

(ii) Which runners will want to take part in these races?

_____

_____   2

[Turn over

[BLANK PAGE]

Marks

3. In the leaflet, there is also information about the Open Day.

Latha Fosgailte airson luchd-spòrs

Disathairne 20 An Lùnastal

A h-uile spòrs an-asgaidh airson an latha.

Feuchaibh lùth-chleasan, sreap is leum-àrd. Bidh na clasaichean airson seo ann fad na maidne.
Bidh trèanadh airson ruith a' gabhail àite bho mheadhan-là gu trì uairean.
Bidh snàmh ann tràth feasgar.
Bidh ball-coise, iomain agus teanas air an cluich a-muigh.

Gheibh sibh na h-uairean uile air a' bhòrd-fiosrachaidh aig an doras.

Ma tha ùidh agaibh ann an spòrs sam bith, rachaibh chun an deasg-fàilteachaidh airson tuilleadh fhaighinn a-mach.

(a) How much will the Open Day cost?

    _____   1

(b) Name **one** of the classes to be held in the morning.

    _____   1

(c) Where is tennis to be played?

    _____   1

(d) Where can the times for the events be found?

    _____

    _____

    _____   3

(e) Where can you get more information about the sporting events?

    _____

    _____   2

Marks

4. Catriona is interested in swimming.

> **Airson snàmh thoiribh leibh deise-snàmh agus dà shearbhadair. Feumaidh ad-snàmh agus glainneachan-snàmh a bhith oirbh cuideachd. Bu chòir aon shearbhadair a bhith agaibh nuair a bhios sibh a-mach agus a-steach às an**  **uisge. Cumaibh am fear eile tioram airson fras aig an deireadh.**
>
> **Na ithibh airson uair a thìde mus bi sibh a' snàmh. Nuair a bhios sibh deiseil, bidh an t-acras agus am pathadh oirbh agus gheibh sibh ceapairean, measan agus deoch.**
>
> **Ma tha sibh airson snàmh a dhèanamh, dèanaibh cinnteach gun cuir sibh ur n-ainmean a-steach dhan oifis sa mhionaid. Chan eil ann ach àiteachan airson còig sgoilearan deug.**

(*a*)   As well as a swimsuit and two towels, what do they need to take for swimming?

_____

_____   2

(*b*)   Why do they need two towels? Give a **detailed** answer.

_____

_____

_____

_____

_____   5

(*c*)   When they are finished, how will they feel?

_____

_____   2

Marks

4.   **(continued)**

(*d*) If the pupils want to swim, what do they have to do immediately?

_____

_____

_____   **3**

(*e*) Why do they have to do this?

_____

_____

_____   **3**

[Turn over

Marks

5. Further information is given about swimming.

> **Trèanadh airson snàmh**
>
> Tha trèanadh gu bhith ann ceithir tursan san t-seachdain, Diluain, Diciadain agus Dihaoine bho leth-uair an dèidh seachd gu cairteal an dèidh ochd anns a' mhadainn. Cuideachd, feasgar Disathairne eadar còig agus sia uairean, bidh cothrom trèanaidh eile ann. Feumaidh sibh a bhith aig a h-uile clas. Nì sibh adhartas ann an ùine ghoirid. Tha sinn an dòchas sgioba sgoinneil fhaighinn.

(*a*) How often are they going to be training?

3

(*b*) Between what times is training during week days?

3

(*c*) What will the effect of all this training be? Give a **detailed** answer.

3

(*d*) What do they hope to get?

2

Marks

6. Information is given about the coaches.

> **Tha mòran eòlais aig na coidsichean a tha
> againn airson na diofar spòrsan. Tha iad air a
> bhith a' dèanamh na h-obrach seo airson
> iomadh bliadhna. Ron seo, bha iad fhèin
> soirbheachail oir bhuannaich iad grunn
> dhuaisean anns na spòrsan aca fhèin.**

(a) What is the first comment made about the coaches for the different
sports?

_____

_____   **2**

(b) How long have they been doing this kind of work?

_____

_____   **2**

(c) What had the coaches achieved in their own sports?

_____

_____

_____   **3**

(60)

[END OF QUESTION PAPER]

[BLANK PAGE]

1240/406

NATIONAL	WEDNESDAY, 28 MAY	GAELIC (LEARNERS)
QUALIFICATIONS	10.30 AM – 11.00 AM	STANDARD GRADE
2008		Credit Level
		Listening Transcript

This paper must not be seen by any candidate.

The material overleaf is provided for use in an emergency only (eg the recording or equipment proving faulty) or where permission has been given in advance by SQA for the material to be read to candidates with additional support needs. The material must be read exactly as printed.

Transcript – Credit Level

Instructions to reader:

For each item, read the English **once**, and then read the Gaelic **three** times with an interval of seven seconds between the readings. On completion of the third reading, pause for the length of time indicated in brackets after each item, to allow the candidates to write their answers.

A Gaelic class in Penifern High School is making a CD for a school in Canada. They are telling about themelves.

Tha clas Gàidhlig ann an Àrd-sgoil Pheighinn Fheàrna a' dèanamh CD airson sgoil ann an Canada. Tha iad ag innse mun deidhinn fhèin.

Kenny speaks first.

Question number one.

What does he say?

Fàilte!

(*20 seconds*)

He gives information about his family.

Question number two.

(*a*)   How many brothers does he have?

Tha dithis bhràithrean agam.

(*20 seconds*)

(*b*)   Where does he come in the family?

Is mise as sine den teaghlach.

(*20 seconds*)

Kenny also has a sister, Anna.

(*c*)   What does she look like?

Tha Anna àrd agus caol.

(*30 seconds*)

Question number three.

What jobs do his parents have?

'S e saor a tha nam athair agus 's e gruagaire a tha nam mhàthair.

(*30 seconds*)

Anna is doing well in school.

Question number four.

(a)   Name the **three** subjects she is particularly good at.

Tha Anna uabhasach math air Beurla, Ceòl agus Cruinn-eòlas.

(40 seconds)

(b)   Where does she want to go when she finishes school?

Tha i ag iarraidh a dhol gu Oilthigh Obar Dheathain.

(30 seconds)

Kenny loves football and is in the local team.

Question number five.

(a)   When and where does Kenny's team train?

Bidh sinn a' trèanadh as t-samhradh aig Pàirc an Rìgh.

(40 seconds)

(b)   How often do they train?

Bidh sinn a' trèanadh uair san t-seachdain.

(30 seconds)

(c)   Where did they finish in the league last year?

Bha sinn anns an treas àite an-uiridh.

(20 seconds)

Aileen is the next to speak. She has just been on holiday.

Question number six.

(a)   Where was she on holiday?

Bha mi anns an Eadailt agus an uair sin anns a' Ghrèig.

(30 seconds)

(b)   Which forms of transport did she use?

An toiseach, ghabh mi plèan agus an dèidh sin chaidh mi air a' bhàt-aiseig.

(30 seconds)

[Turn over

Aileen tells about the second place she visited.

Question number seven.

(*a*)   Where **exactly** was she staying?

Bha mi a' fuireach ann am baile beag ri taobh na mara.

(40 seconds)

(*b*)   Where did she go?

Chaidh mi don tràigh agus do na bùthan.

(30 seconds)

(*c*)   What does she say about the weather? Give a **detailed** answer

Cha robh an t-sìde cho math uaireannan.

(40 seconds)

She makes a final comment.

Question number eight.

What does she say about her holiday, and why?

Chòrd na saor-làithean rium oir bha na daoine càirdeil.

(40 seconds)

The last of the class to speak is Sarah. She loves animals and has lots of pets.

Question number nine.

What pets does she have?

Tha cait agus coin agus eich agam.

(40 seconds)

She describes her favourite pet.

Question number ten.

What is it like?

Tha cù agam le cluasan geala agus earball fada.

(40 seconds)

Sarah also likes cooking and is going to prepare the family meal tonight.

Question number eleven.

What ingredients is she going to use today?

An-diugh, tha mi a' dol a chleachdadh uinneanan, currain agus feòil.

(40 seconds)

Sarah makes a final comment about her family.

Question number twelve.

(*a*)   What does she say about her family?

Tha an teaghlach agam fallain.

(20 seconds)

(*b*)   What do they eat plenty of?

Bidh sinn ag ithe gu leòr mheasan agus ghlasraich.

(30 seconds)

(*c*)   What do they not drink?

Cha bhi sinn ag òl deochan milis.

(20 seconds)

End of test.

Now look over your answers.

[END OF TRANSCRIPT]

[BLANK PAGE]

FOR OFFICIAL USE

C

Total Mark

1240/405

NATIONAL
QUALIFICATIONS
2008

WEDNESDAY, 28 MAY
10.30 AM – 11.00 AM

GAELIC (LEARNERS)
STANDARD GRADE
Credit Level
Listening

Fill in these boxes and read what is printed below.

Full name of centre

Town

Forename(s)

Surname

Date of birth
Day Month Year   Scottish candidate number   Number of seat

Do not open this paper until you are told to do so.

In this test, you have to listen carefully to a number of short passages in Gaelic to find the information asked for in the questions.

You will hear each passage three times, and then you will have time to write your answers. Answer **in English** in the spaces provided.

When you are told to open this paper, read the English introduction at the beginning. Follow the questions printed in the paper as you hear them, and then write your answers. Do not give up the first time you get stuck; leave a blank and keep trying.

As you listen to the passages, you may make notes, but only in this paper.

You are not allowed to leave the examination room until the end of the test.

Before leaving the examination room you must give this book to the invigilator. If you do not, you may lose all the marks for this paper.

DO NOT
WRITE IN
THIS
MARGIN

Marks

A Gaelic class in Penifern High School is making a CD for a school in Canada. They are telling about themselves.

Kenny speaks first.

1. What does he say?

_____   1

*   *   *   *   *

He gives information about his family.

2. (a) How many brothers does he have?

_____   1

(b) Where does he come in the family?

_____   1

Kenny also has a sister, Anna.

(c) What does she look like?

_____

_____   2

*   *   *   *   *

3. What jobs do his parents have?

	Job
Father	
Mother	

2

*   *   *   *   *

Marks

Anna is doing well in school.

4. (*a*)   Name the **three** subjects she is particularly good at.

_____

_____

_____   3

(*b*)   Where does she want to go when she finishes school?

_____

_____   2

*   *   *   *   *

Kenny loves football and is in the local team.

5. (*a*)   When and where does Kenny's team train?

_____

_____

_____   3

(*b*)   How often do they train?

_____

_____   2

(*c*)   Where did they finish in the league last year?

_____   1

*   *   *   *   *

[Turn over

Marks

Aileen is the next to speak. She has just been on holiday.

6. (*a*)   Where was she on holiday?

_____

_____   **2**

(*b*)   Which forms of transport did she use?

_____

_____   **2**

*   *   *   *   *

Aileen tells about the second place she visited.

7. (*a*)   Where **exactly** was she staying?

_____

_____

_____

_____   **4**

(*b*)   Where did she go?

_____

_____   **2**

(*c*)   What does she say about the weather? Give a **detailed** answer.

_____

_____

_____

_____   **4**

*   *   *   *   *

Marks

She makes a final comment.

8. What does she say about her holiday, and why?

_____

_____

_____

_____   **4**

*   *   *   *   *

The last of the class to speak is Sarah. She loves animals and has lots of pets.

9. What pets does she have?

_____

_____

_____   **3**

*   *   *   *   *

She describes her favourite pet.

10. What is it like?

_____

_____

_____

_____   **4**

*   *   *   *   *

[Turn over for Questions 11 and 12 on *Page six*

Marks

Sarah also likes cooking and is going to prepare the family meal tonight.

11. What ingredients is she going to use today?

_____

_____

_____ **3**

*   *   *   *   *

Sarah makes a final comment about her family

12. (*a*) What does she say about her family?

_____ **1**

(*b*) What do they eat plenty of?

_____

_____ **2**

(*c*) What do they not drink?

_____ **1**

*   *   *   *   *

Total marks (50)

[END OF QUESTION PAPER]

STANDARD GRADE | GENERAL | CREDIT

2008

[BLANK PAGE]

G
C

1241/410

NATIONAL
QUALIFICATIONS
2008

WEDNESDAY, 28 MAY
11.15 AM – 12.15 PM

GAELIC (LEARNERS)
STANDARD GRADE
General/Credit Level
(Optional)
Writing

Do not turn over this paper until you are told to do so.

You may use a Gaelic dictionary.

Write your answers in the booklet provided.

Answer, in Gaelic, **two** questions. **One** question must be answered from Section A, and **one** question from Section B. Your answer to Section A should be brief but answer the question, while for Section B more detail is required. To help you write, you have been given checklists, graphics and a suggested way to start each piece.

SECTION A

EITHER

1. Your school is planning a trip to Canada and is arranging to tell you about it.

    Write a **short** letter home, giving information about the trip.

    You should write in sentences and **may** include:

    - the dates of the trip

    - where you are going

    - accommodation

    - activities

    - travel arrangements

    - the cost

    - anything else you want to include.

    Give a suitable beginning and ending.

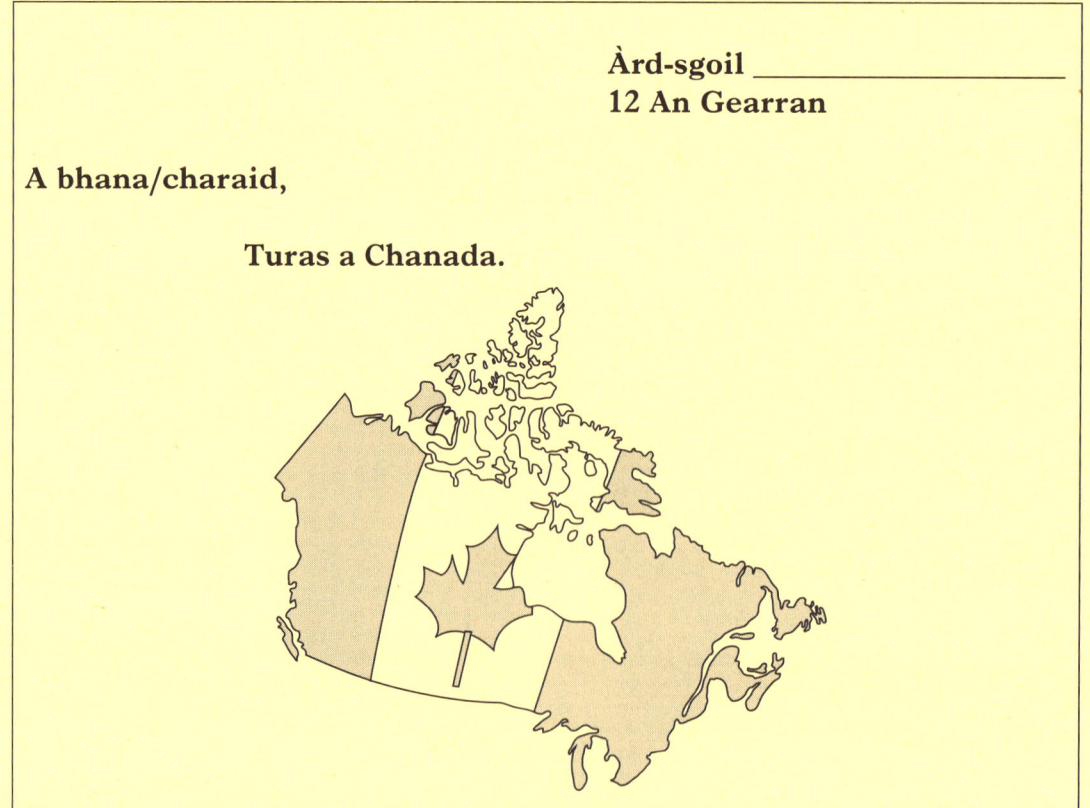

Àrd-sgoil _____
12 An Gearran

A bhana/charaid,

Turas a Chanada.

OR

2.   Your school is holding a fund-raising concert for a trip to Canada.

Write a short article for your school newsletter to advertise the concert.

You should write in sentences and **may** include:

- the day, date and time of the concert

- where it will take place

- who will take part

- what it will cost

- how the money raised will be used

- anything else you want to include.

Consairt Chanada

Tha Àrd-sgoil _____ a' cumail consairt air 6 Am Màrt aig leth-uair an dèidh seachd.

[Turn over for Section B on *Page four*

SECTION B

EITHER

1. You have been on a school trip to Canada and stayed with a family there. Write a diary for one week of your stay.

   You **may** give details of:

   • the village/town where you stayed

   • what your accommodation was like

   • what the family you are staying with was like

   • where you have been

   • what you have done

   • what presents/souvenirs you have bought

   • what ceilidhs/concerts you have been at

   • whether you enjoyed your trip

   • anything else you want to include.

Mo leabhar-latha

Diluain: Tha mi a' fuireach ann am baile beag, brèagha mu fhichead mìle à Halifax. 'S e baile snog a th' ann. An-diugh, bha . . .

OR

2. When you were in Canada, you visited a school. The school wants to gather information about the students who have visited.

You **may** include the following details about yourself:

- your name
- your age
- where you live
- your hobbies
- your family – who they are, their age and what they're like
- what social events there are in your village/town, and where they take place
- what your favourite school subjects are, and why
- what you liked about your stay in Canada, and why
- anything else you want to include.

MISE

'S e Catrìona Chaimbeul an t-ainm a th' orm agus tha mi sia bliadhna deug a dh'aois.

[END OF QUESTION PAPER]

[BLANK PAGE]

[BLANK PAGE]

FOR OFFICIAL USE

G

Total

1240/408

NATIONAL
QUALIFICATIONS
2009

FRIDAY, 29 MAY
2.00 PM – 2.45 PM

GAELIC (LEARNERS)
STANDARD GRADE
General Level
Reading

Fill in these boxes and read what is printed below.

Full name of centre

Town

Forename(s)

Surname

Date of birth
  Day   Month   Year   Scottish candidate number   Number of seat

Do not open this paper until you are told to do so.

When you are told to open the paper, read carefully the English introduction at the beginning, and then work through the paper, starting at Question 1.

When you think you know what to write for each item, write your answer **in English** in the space provided after the item. (You are not expected to fill all the spaces.)

Where boxes like this ☐ are provided, put a tick (✓) in the box beside the answer you think is correct.

You may use a Gaelic dictionary.

You must write any rough work in this paper.

Before leaving the examination room you must give this book to the invigilator. If you do not, you may lose all the marks for this paper.

©

Marks

Amanda is reading a Gaelic newspaper.

1. Amanda reads an article about tourists who visit Scotland.

Luchd-turais ann an Alba

Bha àireamh mhòr de luchd-turais ann an Alba an-uiridh. Thàinig iad à àitean mar an Òlaind, Nirribhidh, a' Bheilg agus a' Ghearmailt. Bha an t-sìde teth agus grianach ach bha i uabhasach fliuch anns an Lùnastal.

(a) What does the article say about the number of tourists in Scotland last year?

It says that there was a lot of ptvarst 1

(b) Name **three** of the countries tourists came from.

Òlaind

Nirribhidh

Ghearmailt   3

(c) In which month was it very wet?

Anns a Lùnastal   1

Marks

2. Amanda continues to read the article.

> **Bha na rathaidean, na trèanaichean agus na plèanaichean uabhasach trang. Bha mòran luchd-turais a' tadhal air na caistealan agus air na h-eileanan. Bha tòrr a' tighinn cuideachd airson goilf a chluich. Bha Dùn Èideann gu sònraichte trang.**

(a) As well as the roads, what were very busy?

_____

_____ 2

(b) What did tourists visit? Tick (✓) **two** places mentioned.

mountains ☐

castles ✓

museums ☐

islands ✓

beaches ☐ 2

(c) Which sport did tourists play?

_____They played Golf_____ 1

(d) Which city was particularly busy? Tick (✓) the **correct** answer.

Edinburgh ✓ Dundee ☐ Glasgow ☐ 1

Marks

3. Amanda reads another article.

> **Turas Sònraichte**
>
> Tha seann trèana a' ruith eadar Malaig agus An Gearastan a h-uile latha. Bidh i a' fàgail aig aon uair deug anns a' mhadainn. Faodaidh sibh ceapairean, deochan, measan agus cèicichean a cheannach air bòrd. Tha àite-suidhe ann airson ochdad. Bidh an trèana a' tilleadh feasgar aig deich mionaidean an dèidh còig.

(*a*) What kind of train is mentioned in the first sentence?

A train that ran though malaig and fort william   1

(*b*) How often does the service run?

Every single day
                                                                                   2

(*c*) What can you buy on board? Name **three** things you can buy.

Sandwiches

drinks

fruit   3

(*d*) How many seats are on the train?

There are 80 seats on board   1

Marks

4. Amanda reads about a new band.

> **Còmhlan Ùr**
>
> Tha an còmhlan ùr seo à Earra-Ghàidheal. Tha dithis nigheanan agus balach anns a' chòmhlan. Tha iad uile ochd deug agus dh'fhàg iad an sgoil am-bliadhna. Bidh iad trang a' siubhal anns an fhoghar. Rinn iad clàr cuideachd. Tha làrach-lìn aca agus tha e glè inntinneach.

(a) Where is the new band from? Tick (✔) the **correct** answer.

Northern Ireland ☐

Argyll ☑

The Borders ☐   1

(b) Who is in the band? Give a **detailed** answer.

There is two girls and one boy on the guitare

3

(c) What will they be busy doing?

They will be entertaining   1

(d) When will they be doing this?

when the leave school   1

(e) What have they made?

1

(f) What is said about their website?

That it is intresesting

2

Marks

5. Amanda then reads an article about a festival.

Fèis Loch Abair

Bidh Fèis Loch Abair a' tòiseachadh am-bliadhna air a' chiad latha den Ghiblean. Thòisich an fhèis seo o chionn naoi bliadhna. Aig an fhèis, bidh clasaichean ann airson clàrsaich, ceòl na fidhle, bocsa-ciùil agus iomain. Faodaidh sibh feuchainn ri òrain a sgrìobhadh agus a sheinn.

(a) When is the festival?

_____

_____ **2**

(b) How many years is it since the festival started?

_____ **1**

(c) Name **three** of the classes which are available.

1 _____

2 _____

3 _____ **3**

(d) What else can you try?

_____

_____

_____ **3**

Marks

6. Another article Amanda reads is about a new development.

Leasachadh Ùr

Tha plana ann airson raon-goilf faisg air Sruighlea. Tha raon 18-tuill, taigh-club, taigh-bìdh, bùth thuathanas agus ionad co-labhairt anns a' phlana. Tha iad an dòchas gum bi e deiseil an-ath-bhliadhna.

(*a*) Where is the new golf course to be?

_____

_____ 2

(*b*) As well as an 18-hole course and clubhouse, what else do they want to build? Tick (✓) **three** correct answers.

Playpark ☐

Restaurant ☐

Farm shop ☐

Ice cream shop ☐

Conference Centre ☐

Hotel ☐

Swimming pool ☐ 3

(*c*) When do they hope it will be ready? Tick (✓) the **correct** answer.

in summer ☐

this year ☐

next year ☐ 1

[Turn over

Marks

7. Finally, Amanda reads an advertisement.

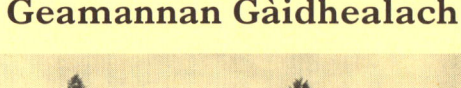

**An t-Achadh Spòrs
Port Rìgh**

**Disathairne 22 An t-Iuchar
Deich uairean**

**Pìobaireachd   Dannsa
Lùth-chleasan**

Biadh

Fealla-dhà gu leòr!

**Ticeadan: Inbhich — còig notaichean
Clann   — leth-phrìs**

(*a*) What event is being advertised?

_____

_____   2

(*b*) Where is this event to be held? Give a **detailed** answer.

_____

_____

_____   3

Marks

7. (continued)

(c) In which month is the event to be held? Tick (✔) the **correct** answer.

May ☐

June ☐

July ☐ **1**

(d) As well as dancing and athletics, what is the other activity?

_____ **1**

(e) What is the cost of an adult ticket?

_____ **1**

(50)

[END OF QUESTION PAPER]

[BLANK PAGE]

G

1240/404

NATIONAL
QUALIFICATIONS
2009

FRIDAY, 29 MAY
9.45 AM – 10.15 AM

GAELIC (LEARNERS)
STANDARD GRADE
General Level
Listening Transcript

This paper must not be seen by any candidate.

The material overleaf is provided for use in an emergency only (eg the recording or equipment proving faulty) or where permission has been given in advance by SQA for the material to be read to candidates with additional support needs. The material must be read exactly as printed.

Transcript – General Level

The pupils of Ardcastle High School are making a film and are recording a commentary for it.

Tha sgoilearan Àrd-sgoil Caisteal na h-Àirde a' cur aithris ri film.

Eilidh starts the commentary for the film.

Question number one.

What does Eilidh say?

Ciamar a tha sibh?

(*20 seconds*)

She is describing a school trip to France.

Question number two.

(*a*)   When did they go? Was it in May, or was it in June, or was it in July? Tick the correct box.

Chaidh sinn don Fhraing anns a' Chèitean.

(*20 seconds*)

Eilidh gives more information.

(*b*)   How did they get there?

Chaidh sinn ann air an trèana agus air a' bhàt-aiseig.

(*30 seconds*)

They were staying in a hotel.

Question number three.

(*a*)   What was it like? Give a **detailed** answer.

Bha e uabhasach mòr agus trang.

(*40 seconds*)

She continues.

(*b*)   What facilities are there in the hotel? Tick the **two** correct boxes.

Bha amar–snàmh agus taigh–dhealbh ann.

(*30 seconds*)

Eilidh describes her hotel room.

(c)   Name **two** of the items of furniture she mentions.

Bha bòrd, preas-aodaich agus lampa ann.

(*30 seconds*)

Eilidh then goes on to talk about the weather.

Question number four.

What was the weather like? Give a **detailed** answer.

Bha i blàth agus tioram.

(*30 seconds*)

John was on the trip to France as well, and he talks about what they did.

Question number five.

(a)   Name **three** of the places they visited.

Chaidh sinn gu eaglais, gu caisteal agus gu taigh-cluiche.

(*40 seconds*)

John continues.

(b)   What did he think of these places?

Bha iad glè inntinneach.

(*30 seconds*)

They met some local teenagers during their trip. John describes one of them, Françoise.

Question number six

(a)   What was she like? Give a **detailed** answer.

Bha i caol le falt donn.

(*40 seconds*)

He also describes what she was wearing.

(b)   What was she wearing?

Bha briogais dhubh agus lèine-t oirre.

(*40 seconds*)

[Turn over

John talks about her family.

Question number seven.

(*a*)   How many brothers does she have?

Tha triùir bhràithrean aice.

(*30 seconds*)

He gives more information about them.

(*b*)   Where do her brothers live?

Tha iad a' fuireach anns a' Chuimrigh.

(*20 seconds*)

Emma was next to talk. She described an outing they went on.

Question number eight.

(*a*)   Where did they go?

Chaidh sinn gu baile beag.

(*30 seconds*)

She gives more information about the outing.

(*b*)   How long did it last? Was it six hours, or was it seven hours, or was it seven days? Tick the correct box.

Bha sinn seachd uairean a thìde air an turas.

(*20 seconds*)

They also went to an open-air market.

Question number nine.

(*a*)   Name the **three** items of food that Emma bought in the market.

Cheannaich mi aran agus càise agus ubhal.

(*40 seconds*)

Emma had these three items for her lunch.

(*b*)   What did she think of them?

Bha iad blasta.

(*20 seconds*)

Emma also bought presents for her family in the market.

Question number ten.

What **two** presents did she buy for her mother? Tick the **two** correct boxes.

Cheannaich mi leabhar agus suiteis do mo mhàthair.

(30 seconds)

At the market, one of the stall-holders asked Emma a question.

Question number eleven.

What did she ask her?

Cò às a tha thu?

(30 seconds)

They all enjoyed the trip to France, and were sad to go home.

Question number twelve.

What day did they arrive home?

Ràinig sinn Dihaoine.

(20 seconds)

Question number thirteen.

What did they say to their teachers when they got back?

Mòran taing!

(30 seconds)

End of test.

Now look over your answers.

[END OF TRANSCRIPT]

[BLANK PAGE]

FOR OFFICIAL USE

G

Total Mark

1240/403

NATIONAL
QUALIFICATIONS
2009

FRIDAY, 29 MAY
9.45 AM – 10.15 AM

GAELIC (LEARNERS)
STANDARD GRADE
General Level
Listening

Fill in these boxes and read what is printed below.

Full name of centre

Town

Forename(s)

Surname

Date of birth
Day Month Year   Scottish candidate number   Number of seat

Do not open this paper until you are told to do so.

In this test, you have to listen carefully to a number of short passages in Gaelic to find the information asked for in the questions.

You will hear each passage three times, and then you will have time to write your answers. Answer **in English** in the spaces provided.

When you are told to open this paper, read the English introduction at the beginning. Follow the questions printed in the paper as you hear them, and then write your answers. Do not give up the first time you get stuck; leave a blank and keep trying.

As you listen to the passages, you may make notes, but only in this paper.

You are not allowed to leave the examination room until the end of the test.

Before leaving the examination room you must give this book to the invigilator. If you do not, you may lose all the marks for this paper.

Marks

The pupils of Ardcastle High School are making a film and are recording a commentary for it.

Eilidh starts the commentary for the film.

1. What does Eilidh say?

_____   **1**

*   *   *   *   *

She is describing a school trip to France.

2. (*a*)   When did they go? Was it in May, or was it in June, or was it in July?

Tick (✓) the correct box.

	(✓)
May	
June	
July	

1

Eilidh gives more information.

(*b*)   How did they get there?

_____

_____   **2**

*   *   *   *   *

Marks

They were staying in a hotel.

3. (*a*)   What was it like? Give a **detailed** answer.

_____

_____

_____   3

She continues.

(*b*)   What facilities are there in the hotel? Tick (✓) the **two** correct boxes.

Restaurant   Swimming-pool   Tennis-court

☐   ☐   ☐

Shop   Cinema

☐   ☐   2

Eilidh describes her hotel room.

(*c*)   Name **two** of the items of furniture she mentions.

1 _____

2 _____   2

*   *   *   *   *

[Turn over

Marks

Eilidh then goes on to talk about the weather.

4. What was the weather like? Give a **detailed** answer.

_____

_____   **2**

*   *   *   *   *

John was on the trip to France as well, and he talks about what they did.

5. (*a*) Name **three** of the places they visited.

1 _____

2 _____

3 _____   **3**

John continues.

(*b*) What did he think of these places?

_____

_____   **2**

*   *   *   *   *

Marks

They met some local teenagers during their trip. John describes one of them, Françoise.

6. (*a*)   What was she like? Give a **detailed** answer.

_____

_____

_____   **3**

He also describes what she was wearing.

(*b*)   What was she wearing?

_____

_____

_____   **3**

*   *   *   *   *

John talks about her family.

7. (*a*)   How many brothers does she have?

_____   **1**

He gives more information about them.

(*b*)   Where do her brothers live?

_____   **1**

*   *   *   *   *

[Turn over

Marks

Emma was next to talk. She described an outing they went on.

8. (*a*) Where did they go?

_____

_____   2

She gives more information about the outing.

(*b*) How long did it last? Was it six hours, or was it seven hours, or was it seven days? Tick (✓) the correct box.

	(✓)
six hours	
seven hours	
seven days	

1

*   *   *   *   *

They also went to an open-air market.

Marks

9. (*a*) Name the **three** items of food that Emma bought in the market.

1 _____

2 _____

3 _____   **3**

Emma had these three items for her lunch.

(*b*) What did she think of them?

_____   **1**

*   *   *   *   *

Emma also bought presents for her family in the market.

10. What **two** presents did she buy for her mother? Tick (✓) the **two** correct boxes.

book   perfume   CD

☐   ☐   ☐

picture   sweets

☐   ☐   **2**

*   *   *   *   *

Turn over for Questions 11, 12 and 13 on *Page eight*

Marks

At the market, one of the stall-holders asked Emma a question.

11. What did she ask her?

_____

_____   2

*   *   *   *   *

They all enjoyed the trip to France, and were sad to go home.

12. What day did they arrive home?

_____   1

*   *   *   *   *

13. What did they say to their teachers when they got back?

_____

_____   2

*   *   *   *   *

Total marks (40)

[END OF QUESTION PAPER]

[BLANK PAGE]

CREDIT GAELIC (LEARNERS) 2009   140   OFFICIAL SQA PAST PAPERS

FOR OFFICIAL USE

C

Total

1240/409

NATIONAL
QUALIFICATIONS
2009

FRIDAY, 29 MAY
3.00 PM – 3.45 PM

GAELIC (LEARNERS)
STANDARD GRADE
Credit Level
Reading

Fill in these boxes and read what is printed below.

Full name of centre

Town

Forename(s)

Surname

Date of birth
Day Month Year

Scottish candidate number

Number of seat

Do not open this paper until you are told to do so.

When you think you know what to write for each item, write your answer **in English** in the space provided after the item. (You are not expected to fill all the spaces.)

You may use a Gaelic dictionary.

You must write any rough work in this paper.

Before leaving the examination room you must give this book to the invigilator. If you do not, you may lose all the marks for this paper.

Marks

Iain bought a Gaelic newspaper.

1.   One of the articles is about a crime.

> **Mèirle ann am Muile**
>
> **Bhris robairean a-steach dhan àrd-sgoil ann am Muile aig an deireadh-sheachdain.   Ghoid iad coimpiutairean agus innealan-ciùil agus uidheaman-spòrs.**
>
> **Thuirt an ceannard, Mgr. Peutan, gun robh e glè dhuilich oir bha fiach fichead mìle not air a ghoid. Bha e ag iarraidh air daoine fònadh a-steach le fiosrachadh mun seo.**
>
> **Tha na poilis a' coimhead airson triùir dheugairean.**

(*a*)   Where did this crime happen?

_____   1

(*b*)   What building was broken into?

_____   1

(*c*)   When did this happen?

_____   1

(*d*)   Name **one** of the items stolen.

_____   1

(*e*)   Who is Mr Beaton?

_____   1

(*f*)   What was the value of the items stolen?

_____

_____   2

(*g*)   Who are the police looking for?

_____

_____   2

Marks

2. Iain reads about a road accident.

> **Tubaist Rathaid**
>
> **Feasgar an-dè, bha tubaist air an rathad faisg air a' Ghearastan. Bhuail dà làraidh na chèile agus chaidh dithis a thoirt don ospadal. Bhris fireannach a chas agus gheàrr boireannach a làmh.   Bha uisge trom ann fad an latha agus bha na rathaidean fliuch. B' e seo an treas tubaist air an rathad seo air a' mhìos seo. Tha daoine ag ràdh gu bheil an rathad cunnartach agus gu bheil dràibhearan a' dol ro luath. Bha an rathad dùinte airson còrr is uair a thìde.**

(*a*)   Where did the road accident occur?

_____

_____   2

(*b*)   (i) Describe the man's injuries.

_____

_____   2

(ii) Describe the woman's injuries.

_____

_____   2

(*c*)   What was the weather like?

_____

_____   2

(*d*)   What do people say about the road?

_____   1

(*e*)   What do they say about drivers?

_____

_____

_____   3

Marks

3. Another article is about a hotel.

An Taigh-òsta Rìoghail

Tha an Taigh-òsta Rìoghail a' fosgladh an-ath-sheachdain an dèidh a bhith dùinte airson bliadhna. Chosg a' chompanaidh millean not a' dèanamh suas taobh a-staigh agus taobh a-muigh an taigh-òsta.

Tha na rumannan mòr agus spaideil le eadar-lìon, telebhisean agus frids. Anns an rùm-bìdh, gheibh sibh biadh à Alba. Tha tòrr den bhiadh a' tighinn às an sgìre – mar iasg, feòil-caorach, sitheann agus glasraich.

(*a*) When is the hotel opening?

_____

_____   **2**

(*b*) What was one million pounds spent on?

_____

_____

_____   **3**

(*c*) What is in each room?

_____

_____

_____   **3**

(*d*) Name **three** of the foods which are sourced locally.

_____

_____

_____   **3**

Marks

4. Another article is about a concert.

> **Bha consairt ann an Talla a' Bhaile, ann an Inbhir Nis, feasgar Dihaoine. Bha sgoilearan a bha math ann an ceòl traidiseanta a' gabhail pàirt. Bha consairt sgoinneil ann le seinn, pìobaireachd, fidhlearachd agus dealbh-chluich èibhinn. Chuir sgoilearan air dòigh an consairt le cuideachadh bho na tidsearan agus na pàrantan aca. Thog iad faisg air mìle gu leth not airson ospadal ùr ann an Afraga.**

(*a*) Where was the concert held?

_____

_____

_____   3

(*b*) Which pupils took part in the concert?

_____

_____

_____   3

(*c*) As well as singing, name two other things that were performed.

_____

_____   2

(*d*) What was the reason for raising money?

_____

_____

_____   3

[Turn over

Marks

5. One article Iain reads is about a competition.

Farpais Tàileisg

An t-seachdain seo chaidh, bha coinneamh san Òban airson cluicheadairean tàileisg. Bha còrr is dà cheud cluicheadair a' cluich bho Dihaoine gu Là na Sàbaid. Is ann à Alba bha a' mhòr-chuid aca ach bha farpaisich ann à Sasainn, Èirinn agus an Òlaind cuideachd.

Thàinig na teaghlaichean còmhla ris na farpaisich agus chòrd an deireadh-sheachdain ris a h-uile duine. Bha an t-sìde uabhasach brèagha cuideachd. Bhuannaich Raibeart Grannd à Pàislig a' phrìomh dhuais.

Bha a' chiad fharpais tàileisg san Òban o chionn còig bliadhna deug.

(*a*)   What competition was taking place in Oban?

_____   1

(*b*)   When was the competition?

_____

_____   2

(*c*)   As well as Scotland and Ireland, where did the other players come from?

_____

_____   2

(*d*)   Who accompanied the competitors?

_____   1

(*e*)   When did this competition first take place in Oban?

_____

_____   2

Marks

6.   Iain reads about a swimming event.

Snàmhadair à Leòdhas

Bhuannaich Anndra Camshron, a tha còig bliadhna deug, dà dhuais airson snàmh. Fhuair e a' chiad duais agus an dàrna duais aig farpaisean na sgìre anns a' Chèitean. Anns an Lùnastal, bidh e a' dol air adhart gu prìomh fharpais na h-Alba airson òigridh, ann an Dùn Èideann.

Bha Anndra uabhasach toilichte leis na duaisean aige. Thuirt an coidse gun robh Anndra ag obair cruaidh. Bidh e a' trèanadh a h-uile latha agus bidh e daonnan a' feuchainn ri snàmh nas luaithe. Bidh Anndra a' trèanadh ceithir tursan san t-seachdain.

(a)   What two prizes did Andrew Cameron win?

_____

_____   2

(b)   When was the swimming event held?

_____   1

(c)   What competition is taking place in Edinburgh in August?

_____

_____

_____   3

(d)   How does Andrew feel about his success?

_____

_____   2

(e)   What does Andrew always try to do in training?

_____   1

(60)

[END OF QUESTION PAPER]

[BLANK PAGE]

C

1240/406

NATIONAL
QUALIFICATIONS
2009

FRIDAY, 29 MAY
10.30 AM – 11.00 AM

GAELIC (LEARNERS)
STANDARD GRADE
Credit Level
Listening Transcript

This paper must not be seen by any candidate.

The material overleaf is provided for use in an emergency only (eg the recording or equipment proving faulty) or where permission has been given in advance by SQA for the material to be read to candidates with additional support needs. The material must be read exactly as printed.

Transcript – Credit Level

The pupils of Ardcastle High School are making a film and are recording a commentary for it.

Tha sgoilearan Àrd-sgoil Caisteal na h-Àirde a' cur aithris ri film.

Ross is introducing this section, which contains information for and about tourists.

Question number one.

(*a*)   What does Ross say at the start of this section?

Fàilte!

(*20 seconds*)

Ross talks about the tourists who come to Ardcastle.

(*b*)   Name the **three** countries he mentions.

Thig iad ann às a' Ghearmailt, às an Fhraing agus às na Stàitean Aonaichte.

(*40 seconds*)

Ross goes on to talk about the accommodation in the area.

Question number two.

(*a*)   What is the name, in English, of the biggest hotel?

'S e "Taigh an Eilein" ainm an taigh-òsta as motha.

(*30 seconds*)

(*b*)   Where, **exactly**, is it?

Tha e ri taobh talla a' bhaile.

(*30 seconds*)

He continues.

(*c*)   How many rooms does the hotel have?

(*d*)   What are the rooms like?

Tha mu fhichead rùm anns an taigh-òsta, agus tha iad cofhurtail agus spaideil.

(*40 seconds*)

Ross goes on to talk about a ceilidh the hotel puts on for tourists. He tells us about one of the performers.

Question number three.

(*a*)   Who is the main performer at the ceilidh?

'S e Ealasaid NicDhòmhnaill an t-ainm a th' oirre.

(*30 seconds*)

This performer talks to the audience.

(*b*)   What question did the performer ask the audience?

A bheil Gàidhlig agaibh?

(*30 seconds*)

(*c*)   What did this performer do at the ceilidh? Give a **detailed** answer.

Bha i a' seinn agus a' cluich na clàrsaich. Tha i math oirre.

(*40 seconds*)

Ross hands over to Eilidh, who is going to talk about activities for tourists in the area.

Question number four.

What **three** activities does Eilidh mention?

Faodaidh sibh sreap, marcachd agus seòladh.

(*40 seconds*)

Eilidh describes Ben More, the hill above Ardcastle.

Question number five.

(*a*)   What height, in metres, is Ben More? Give a **detailed** answer.

Tha i faisg air mìle meatair a dh'àirde.

(*40 seconds*)

She continues.

(*b*)   What can you see from the top of Ben More?

Chì thu a' mhuir agus Uibhist a Deas bho mhullach na beinne.

(*40 seconds*)

[**Turn over**

Eilidh gives the tourists some advice about outdoor activities.

(c)   What is the first piece of information they must leave?

Feumaidh sibh innse càit a bheil sibh a' dol.

(*30 seconds*)

(d)   What is the second piece of information they must leave?

Feumaidh sibh innse cuin a tha sibh a' tilleadh.

(*30 seconds*)

Eilidh now hands over to Emma, who starts talking about a shop that makes chocolate.

Question number six.

(a)   What price is each individual chocolate?

Cosgaidh iad fichead sgillinn 's a naoi an tè.

(*30 seconds*)

Emma gives more information about the chocolates.

(b)   Apart from cocoa, name **two** of the main ingredients.

Bidh iad a' cur siùcar, uachdar agus cnothan annta.

(*30 seconds*)

Emma then talks about the castle in Ardcastle, which tourists like to visit.

Question number seven.

(a)   How do you get to the castle from the hotel? Give a **detailed** answer.

Theirig sìos an rathad agus theirig don làimh chlì.

(*40 seconds*)

She tells us more about the castle.

(b)   What does she say?

Tha e nas motha na Caisteal Inbhir Nis.

(*30 seconds*)

She continues.

(c)   How old is the castle?

Tha e ochd ceud bliadhna a dh'aois.

(*40 seconds*)

John is going to complete the information for tourists by talking about the weather.

Question number eight.

What comment does John make about the weather? Give a **detailed** answer.

Uaireannan tha e ro theth airson a bhith a' coiseachd!

(40 seconds)

The film concludes.

Question number nine.

What does John say at the end?

Thigibh an-seo!

(30 seconds)

End of test.

Now look over your answers.

[END OF TRANSCRIPT]

[BLANK PAGE]

FOR OFFICIAL USE

C

Total Mark

1240/405

NATIONAL
QUALIFICATIONS
2009

FRIDAY, 29 MAY
10.30 AM – 11.00 AM

GAELIC (LEARNERS)
STANDARD GRADE
Credit Level
Listening

Fill in these boxes and read what is printed below.

Full name of centre

Town

Forename(s)

Surname

Date of birth
Day Month Year

Scottish candidate number

Number of seat

Do not open this paper until you are told to do so.

In this test, you have to listen carefully to a number of short passages in Gaelic to find the information asked for in the questions.

You will hear each passage three times, and then you will have time to write your answers. Answer **in English** in the spaces provided.

When you are told to open this paper, read the English introduction at the beginning. Follow the questions printed in the paper as you hear them, and then write your answers. Do not give up the first time you get stuck; leave a blank and keep trying.

As you listen to the passages, you may make notes, but only in this paper.

You are not allowed to leave the examination room until the end of the test.

Before leaving the examination room you must give this book to the invigilator. If you do not, you may lose all the marks for this paper.

DO NOT
WRITE IN
THIS
MARGIN

The pupils of Ardcastle High School are making a film and are recording a commentary for it.

Marks

Ross is introducing this section, which contains information for and about tourists.

1. (*a*) What does Ross say at the start of this section?

_____   **1**

Ross talks about the tourists who come to Ardcastle.

(*b*) Name the **three** countries he mentions.

1 _____

2 _____

3 _____   **3**

*   *   *   *   *

Ross goes on to talk about the accommodation in the area.

2. (*a*) What is the name, in English, of the biggest hotel?

_____

_____   **2**

(*b*) Where, **exactly**, is it?

_____

_____   **2**

He continues.

(*c*) How many rooms does the hotel have?

_____

_____   **2**

(*d*) What are the rooms like?

_____

_____   **2**

*   *   *   *   *

Marks

Ross goes on to talk about a ceilidh the hotel puts on for tourists. He tells us about one of the performers.

3. (*a*)   Who is the main performer at the ceilidh?

_____

_____   2

This performer talks to the audience.

(*b*)   What question did the performer ask the audience?

_____

_____   2

(*c*)   What did this performer do at the ceilidh? Give a **detailed** answer.

_____

_____

_____   3

*   *   *   *   *

Ross hands over to Eilidh, who is going to talk about activities for tourists in the area.

4.   What **three** activities does Eilidh mention?

1 _____

2 _____

3 _____   3

*   *   *   *   *

[Turn over

Marks

Eilidh describes Ben More, the hill above Ardcastle.

5. (*a*)   What height, in metres, is Ben More? Give a **detailed** answer.

_____

_____

_____   3

She continues.

(*b*)   What can you see from the top of Ben More?

_____

_____

_____   3

Eilidh gives the tourists some advice about outdoor activities.

(*c*)   What is the first piece of information they must leave?

_____

_____   2

(*d*)   What is the second piece of information they must leave?

_____

_____   2

*   *   *   *   *

Marks

Eilidh now hands over to Emma, who starts talking about a shop that makes chocolate.

6. (*a*) What price is each individual chocolate?

_____

_____   2

Emma gives more information about the chocolates.

(*b*) Apart from cocoa, name **two** of the main ingredients.

1 _____

2 _____   2

*   *   *   *   *

Emma then talks about the castle in Ardcastle, which tourists like to visit.

7. (*a*) How do you get to the castle from the hotel? Give a **detailed** answer.

_____

_____

_____

_____   4

She tells us more about the castle.

(*b*) What does she say?

_____

_____   2

She continues.

(*c*) How old is the castle?

_____

_____

_____   3

*   *   *   *   *

[Turn over for Questions 8 and 9 on *Page six*

Marks

John is going to complete the information for tourists by talking about the weather.

8. What comment does John make about the weather? Give a **detailed** answer.

_____

_____

_____   3

*   *   *   *   *

The film concludes.

9. What does John say at the end?

_____

_____   2

*   *   *   *   *

Total marks (50)

[END OF QUESTION PAPER]

[BLANK PAGE]

G
C

1241/410

NATIONAL
QUALIFICATIONS
2009

FRIDAY, 29 MAY
11.15 AM – 12.15 PM

GAELIC (LEARNERS)
STANDARD GRADE
General/Credit Level
(Optional)
Writing

Do not turn over this paper until you are told to do so.

You may use a Gaelic dictionary.

Write your answers in the booklet provided.

Answer, in Gaelic, <u>two</u> questions. <u>One</u> question must be answered from Section A, and <u>one</u> question from Section B. Your answer to Section A should be brief but answer the question, while for Section B more detail is required. To help you write, you have been given checklists, graphics and a suggested way to start each piece.

SECTION A

EITHER

1. You have been asked to write a fact-file about yourself for a writing competition. In it, you have to write a short description of yourself under the heading **"Mise"**.

    You **may** include:

    • your name

    • your age

    • your family

    • where you live, and what it's like

    • your likes and dislikes

    • any other relevant information.

Mise

Is mise Anna agus tha mi . . .

OR

2.   You're on a school trip. Write a diary entry for **one** day of your trip.

You **may** give details of:

- where you are

- what your accommodation is like

- what you did that day

- what the weather was like

- what you think of it all

- any other relevant information.

Turas-sgoile

Dimàirt: **Tha sinn ann an Lunnainn agus tha sinn a' fuireach ann an . . .**

[Turn over for Section B on *Page four*

SECTION B

EITHER

1.   Your school has advised you to write a CV or Personal Statement about yourself for when you apply for a job or further education. They have suggested you include information that an employer/college would want to know about you.

In your CV or Personal Statement, you **may** include:

- your name

- your age

- the school you go to

- the subjects you are doing

- what your favourite subjects are, and why

- your pastimes, and why you like doing them

- what you did for your work-experience and whether you enjoyed it

- any other relevant information.

Anna NicRath

'S e Anna NicRath an t-ainm a th' orm, agus tha mi . . .

OR

2. A group of pupils from abroad visited your school, and one of them stayed with you. You have been asked to write an article about their visit for your school magazine.

    You **may** include in your article:

    *   where the pupils were from
    *   how long the group were here for
    *   what the group did
    *   who was staying with you
    *   how old s/he was
    *   what s/he was like (appearance and personality)
    *   what kind of music s/he liked
    *   what presents s/he bought
    *   any other relevant information.

Sgoilearan bhon Fhraing

Bha sgoilearan bhon Fhraing anns an sgoil againn. Bha iad an seo airson . . .

[END OF QUESTION PAPER]

[BLANK PAGE]

STANDARD GRADE | GENERAL

2010

[BLANK PAGE]

FOR OFFICIAL USE

G

Total

1240/408

NATIONAL
QUALIFICATIONS
2010

THURSDAY, 20 MAY
2.00 PM – 2.45 PM

GAELIC (LEARNERS)
STANDARD GRADE
General Level
Reading

Fill in these boxes and read what is printed below.

Full name of centre

Town

Forename(s)

Surname

Date of birth
Day   Month   Year   Scottish candidate number   Number of seat

Do not open this paper until you are told to do so.

When you are told to open the paper, read carefully the English introduction at the beginning, and then work through the paper, starting at Question 1.

When you think you know what to write for each item, write your answer **in English** in the space provided after the item. (You are not expected to fill all the spaces.)

Where boxes like this ☐ are provided, put a tick (✓) in the box beside the answer you think is correct.

You may use a Gaelic dictionary.

You must write any rough work in this paper.

Before leaving the examination room you must give this book to the Invigilator. If you do not, you may lose all the marks for this paper.

Marks

As part of their course, students are expected to produce pieces of writing.

1. Fiona writes about her school day.

Bidh mi ag èirigh aig seachd uairean. Cha toigh leam a bhith ag èirigh tràth oir tha mi uabhasach leisg. Gabhaidh mi fras ro mo bhracaist agus, airson bracaist, bidh mi ag ithe gràn bracaist agus sùgh mheasan. Feumaidh mi an taigh fhàgail aig fichead mionaid gu naoi. Bidh mi a' coiseachd dhan sgoil còmhla ri mo bhràthair.

(*a*) When does Fiona get up?

_____   1

(*b*) Why does she not like getting up early?

_____

_____   2

(*c*) When does she have a shower?

Tick (✓) the correct answer.

Before breakfast   ☐

After breakfast   ☐

At 8 o'clock   ☐   1

DO NOT WRITE IN THIS MARGIN

Marks

1. (continued)

(*d*) What does she have for breakfast?

Tick (✓) the **two** correct answers.

Tea	☐
Cereal	☐
Fruit juice	☐
Toast	☐
Bacon	☐

2

(*e*) How does she go to school?

______________________________ **1**

(*f*) Who goes to school with her?

______________________________ **1**

[Turn over

Marks

2.   Eilidh writes about her sister.

Tha mo phiuthar, Ealasaid, sia bliadhna deug agus tha i air an t-siathamh bliadhna anns an sgoil. Tha i ag iarraidh a dhol don oilthigh an-ath-bhliadhna. Tha i math air giotàr agus clàrsach a chluich. Tha i nas fheàrr air a' chlàrsaich oir thòisich i ga cluich nuair a bha i anns a' bhun-sgoil. Is toigh leatha a bhith a' bèicearachd agus a' cadal cuideachd.

(a) How old is her sister?

_____   1

(b) When does she want to go to university?

_____

_____   2

(c) Which instruments does she play?

_____

_____   2

(d) When did she start playing the instrument she is better at?

_____   1

(e) What else does her sister like doing?

_____

_____   2

DO NOT
WRITE IN
THIS
MARGIN

Marks

3. Iain writes about his long weekend.

Dihaoine, tha mi a' dol a Dhùn Èideann airson an deireadh-sheachdain. Tha mi a' dol a dh'fhuireach còmhla ri mo cho-ogha Raonaid. Tha i a' fuireach ri taobh pàirc. Chan eil i fada bho mheadhan a' bhaile.

Disathairne, anns a' mhadainn, tha mi ag iarraidh a dhol a dh'fhaicinn an oilthigh. Feasgar, thèid sinn gu gèam rugbaidh. Tha Alba a' cluich na Frainge aig Pàirc Murrayfield. Tillidh mi dhachaigh Diluain.

(*a*) When is Iain going to Edinburgh?

_____ 1

(*b*) Who is Iain going to stay with? Give a **detailed** answer.

_____

_____ 2

(*c*) Where does this person live?

_____

_____ 2

(*d*) When is Iain going to see the university?

_____

_____ 2

(*e*) Who are Scotland playing at rugby?

_____ 1

(*f*) What is happening on Monday?

_____

_____ 2

Marks

4.   Martin writes about himself.

Is mise Màrtainn MacDhòmhnaill. Tha mi air an treas bliadhna anns an àrd-sgoil. Tha mi a' dèanamh ochd cuspairean anns an sgoil. Is toigh leam Cruinn-èolas ach cha toigh leam idir Eachdraidh. Is toigh leam a bhith a' faicinn mo charaidean anns an sgoil. Tha na tidsearan math.

(*a*)   What is Martin's surname?

_____   1

(*b*)   What year, in school, is he in?

_____   1

(*c*)   How many subjects is he doing?

_____   1

(*d*)   What two things does Martin like?

   Tick (✓) the **two** correct answers.

   English   ☐

   Geography   ☐

   School food   ☐

   Seeing his friends   ☐

   Homework   ☐

   History   ☐   2

Marks

5. Simon writes about the weather.

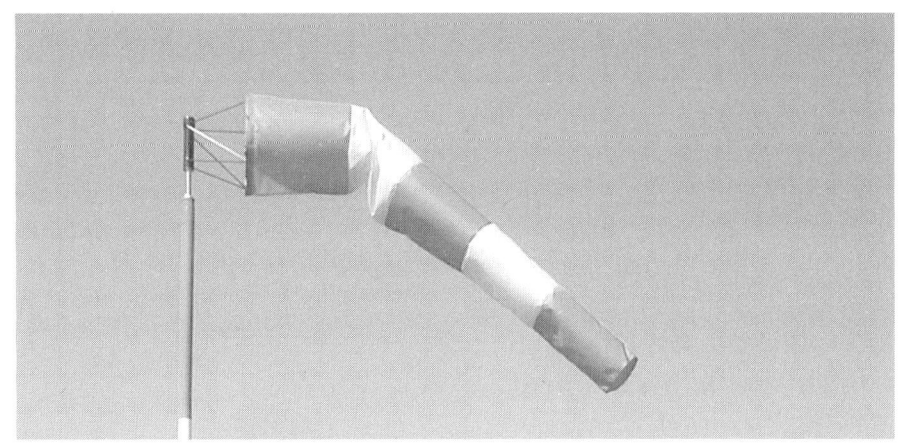

An Giblean – Bha i grianach anns a' Ghiblean. Cha robh mòran uisge ann.

An Cèitean – Bha i fliuch agus fuar. Bha i nas blàithe an cola-deug mu dheireadh.

(*a*) What was the weather like in April?

_____ 1

(*b*) What is said about the rainfall?

_____

_____ 2

(*c*) What was the weather like in May?

_____

_____ 2

(*d*) What is said about the weather in the last fortnight?

_____ 1

[Turn over

DO NOT WRITE IN THIS MARGIN

Marks

6. Anna adds the following job advertisement.

> ## Obair anns an taigh-dhealbh
>
> **Freagarrach airson sgoilear**
>
> **A' reic reòiteagan is suiteis**
> **Dihaoine agus Disathairne**
>
> **Ma tha ùidh agad san obair,**
> **fòn an taigh-dhealbh agus bruidhinn ri Anndra.**

(*a*) Where is the work?

_____ 1

(*b*) Who would this job suit?

_____ 1

(*c*) Describe the work involved.

_____

_____

_____ 3

(*d*) If you are interested in the job, what are you told to do?

_____

_____

_____ 3

DO NOT WRITE IN THIS MARGIN

Marks

7. Susan has made a matching exercise using phrases.

Match the phrases in Gaelic with the English phrases shown in the table below. Write the correct number in the spaces provided. One has been done for you.

a Tha mi deiseil.   1 I am tired.

b Tha mi duilich.   2 I am sorry.

c Chan eil mi a' tuigsinn.   3 I don't understand.

d Tha mi trang.   4 I am finished.

e Tha mi sgìth.   5 I am happy.

f Tha mi toilichte.   6 I am busy.

a	4
b	
c	
d	
e	
f	

5

(50)

[END OF QUESTION PAPER]

[BLANK PAGE]

G

1240/404

NATIONAL
QUALIFICATIONS
2010

THURSDAY, 20 MAY
9.45 AM – 10.15 AM

GAELIC (LEARNERS)
STANDARD GRADE
General Level
Listening Transcript

This paper must not be seen by any candidate.

The material overleaf is provided for use in an emergency only (eg the recording or equipment proving faulty) or where permission has been given in advance by SQA for the material to be read to candidates with additional support needs. The material must be read exactly as printed.

Transcript—General Level

> **Instructions to reader:**
>
> For each item, read the English **once**, and then read the Gaelic **three** times with an interval of seven seconds between the readings. On completion of the third reading, pause for the length of time indicated in brackets after each item, to allow the candidates to write their answers.

The Fourth Year pupils of Glenbeg High School are reading letters from their Canadian pen pals.

Tha sgoilearan na Ceathramh Bliadhna ann an Àrd-sgoil a' Ghlinne Bhig a' leughadh litrichean bho na caraidean-pinn aca à Canada.

Neil is reading a letter from his Canadian pen pal, Cody.

Cody is describing where he lives.

Question number one.

What is his town like?

'S e baile beag a th' ann.

(20 seconds)

He gives more information.

Question number two.

(a)   How many people live there? Is it 3,000, or is it 4,000, or is it 5,000? Tick the correct box.

Tha còig mìle duine a' fuireach ann.

(20 seconds)

He continues.

(b)   What can you see near his town?

Chì thu lochan agus beanntan faisg air a' bhaile agam.

(30 seconds)

Cody is learning Gaelic in school, and gets help from his Gaelic-speaking granny.

Question number three.

Where is his granny from?

'S ann à Leòdhas a tha mo sheanmhair.

(20 seconds)

Cody likes to play ice-hockey.

Question number four.

(a)   On what **two** days does he play ice-hockey?

Bidh mi a' cluich Dimàirt agus Dihaoine.

(30 seconds)

His team took part in a competition recently.

(b)   Where were they placed in this competition?

Bha sinn anns an treas àite.

(20 seconds)

The team had a meal after the competition.

(c)   Name **three** of the things they ate.

Ghabh sinn brot le aran, agus feòil agus glasraich.

(40 seconds)

Cody continues.

(d)   Where did they stay after the competition?

Bha sinn a' fuireach ann an ostail-òigridh mhòr.

(30 seconds)

(e)   How many were in each room?

Bha sianar anns gach rùm.

(20 seconds)

Cody makes a comment about the competition.

(f)   What comment does he make? Give a **detailed** answer.

Chòrd i rium gu mòr.

(30 seconds)

[Turn over

Calum is reading a letter from his pen pal, Ethan. Ethan describes his holiday in Scotland.

Question number five.

(*a*)   Which city was he staying in?

Bha mi a' fuireach ann an Inbhir Nis.

(*20 seconds*)

(*b*)   What **three** things did he do while he was there?

Bha mi ag iasgach, a' coiseachd agus a' sreap.

(*40 seconds*)

(*c*)   How long was he in Scotland?

Bha mi ann airson mìos.

(*20 seconds*)

Màiri reads the letter from her pen pal, Emma. Emma describes a concert held recently in her school.

Question number six.

(*a*)   How many dollars did the tickets cost?

Bha na tiogaidean ochd dolairean.

(*20 seconds*)

(*b*)   What did the compere say at the start of the concert?

Fàilte!

(*20 seconds*)

Emma mentions three of the items in the concert.

(*c*)   Name the **three** items.

Bha daoine a' seinn, a' cluich a' bhogsa agus a' dannsadh.

(*40 seconds*)

Emma continues.

(*d*)   When did the concert finish?

Bha e deiseil aig leth-uair an dèidh deich.

(*30 seconds*)

(*e*)   How much did they make at the concert? Was it $500, or was it $600, or was it $700? Tick the correct box.

Rinn iad seachd ceud dolair.

(*20 seconds*)

The last letter is from Mary-Jane, and Kirsty is reading it to the others. She is talking about her youth-club.

Question number seven.

Where is the youth club held?

Tha e ga chumail anns an talla.

(20 seconds)

The youth club has been doing a sponsored swim.

Question number eight.

(*a*)   Who were they raising the money for?

Tha an t-airgead a' dol gu clann ann an Afraga.

(30 seconds)

Mary-Jane injured herself during the sponsored swim.

(*b*)   Did she injure her knee, or her leg, or her shoulder? Tick the correct box.

Ghoirtich mi mo chas.

(20 seconds)

Another member of Mary-Jane's family took part in the sponsored swim.

Question number nine.

(*a*)   Which member of Mary-Jane's family took part?

Bha mo bhràthair a' snàmh.

(30 seconds)

(*b*)   What does this family member look like? Give a **detailed** answer.

Tha e àrd agus caol le sùilean gorma.

(40 seconds)

All the pen pals are planning to keep in touch.

Question number ten.

How do they plan to keep in touch?

Air an eadar-lìon agus le fòn-làimhe.

(30 seconds)

End of test.

Now look over your answers.

[END OF TRANSCRIPT]

[BLANK PAGE]

FOR OFFICIAL USE

G

Total
Mark

1240/403

NATIONAL
QUALIFICATIONS
2010

THURSDAY, 20 MAY
9.45 AM – 10.15 AM

GAELIC (LEARNERS)
STANDARD GRADE
General Level
Listening

Fill in these boxes and read what is printed below.

Full name of centre

Town

Forename(s)

Surname

Date of birth
Day   Month   Year   Scottish candidate number   Number of seat

Do not open this paper until you are told to do so.

In this test, you have to listen carefully to a number of short passages in Gaelic to find the information asked for in the questions.

You will hear each passage three times, and then you will have time to write your answers. Answer **in English** in the spaces provided.

When you are told to open this paper, read the English introduction at the beginning. Follow the questions printed in the paper as you hear them, and then write your answers. Do not give up the first time you get stuck; leave a blank and keep trying.

As you listen to the passages, you may make notes, but only in this paper.

You are not allowed to leave the examination room until the end of the test.

Before leaving the examination room you must give this book to the Invigilator. If you do not, you may lose all the marks for this paper.

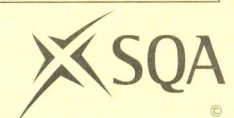

Marks

The Fourth Year pupils of Glenbeg High School are reading letters from their Canadian pen pals.

Neil is reading a letter from his Canadian pen pal, Cody.

Cody is describing where he lives.

1. What is his town like?

_____   1

*   *   *   *   *

He gives more information.

2. (*a*) How many people live there? Is it 3,000, or is it 4,000, or is it 5,000?

Tick (✓) the correct box.

	(✓)
3,000	
4,000	
5,000	

1

He continues.

(*b*) What can you see near his town?

_____

_____   2

*   *   *   *   *

Cody is learning Gaelic in school, and gets help from his Gaelic-speaking granny.

3. Where is his granny from?

_____   1

*   *   *   *   *

Marks

Cody likes to play ice-hockey.

4. (*a*)   On what **two** days does he play ice-hockey?

_____

_____   2

His team took part in a competition recently.

(*b*)   Where were they placed in this competition?

_____   1

The team had a meal after the competition.

(*c*)   Name **three** of the things they ate.

_____

_____

_____   3

Cody continues.

(*d*)   Where did they stay after the competition?

_____

_____   2

(*e*)   How many were in each room?

_____   1

Cody makes a comment about the competition.

(*f*)   What comment does he make? Give a **detailed** answer.

_____

_____   2

*   *   *   *   *

[Turn over

Marks

Calum is reading a letter from his pen pal, Ethan. Ethan describes his holiday in Scotland.

5. (*a*) Which city was he staying in?

_____ 1

(*b*) What **three** things did he do while he was there?

_____

_____

_____ 3

(*c*) How long was he in Scotland?

_____ 1

* * * * *

Màiri reads the letter from her pen pal, Emma. Emma describes a concert held recently in her school.

6. (*a*) How many dollars did the tickets cost?

_____ 1

(*b*) What did the compere say at the start of the concert?

_____ 1

* * * * *

Emma mentions three of the items in the concert.

(c)   Name the **three** items.

_____

_____

_____   3

Emma continues

(d)   When did the concert finish?

_____

_____   2

(e)   How much did they make at the concert? Was it $500, or was it $600, or was it $700? Tick (✓) the correct box.

	(✓)
$500	
$600	
$700	

   1

*   *   *   *   *

[Turn over

Marks

The last letter is from Mary-Jane, and Kirsty is reading it to the others. She is talking about her youth-club.

7. Where is the youth-club held?

_____   1

* * * * *

The youth-club has been doing a sponsored swim.

8. (*a*) Who were they raising the money for?

_____

_____   2

Mary-Jane injured herself during the sponsored swim.

(*b*) Did she injure her knee, or her leg, or her shoulder? Tick (✓) the correct box.

	(✓)
knee	
leg	
shoulder	

1

* * * * *

Marks

Another member of Mary-Jane's family took part in the sponsored swim.

9. (*a*)   Which member of Mary-Jane's family took part?

_____   **1**

(*b*)   What does this family member look like? Give a **detailed** answer.

_____

_____

_____

_____   **4**

*　*　*　*　*

All the pen pals are planning to keep in touch.

10. How do they plan to keep in touch?

_____

_____   **2**

*　*　*　*　*

Total marks (40)

[END OF QUESTION PAPER]

[BLANK PAGE]

[BLANK PAGE]

FOR OFFICIAL USE

C

Total

1240/409

NATIONAL	THURSDAY, 20 MAY	**GAELIC (LEARNERS)**
QUALIFICATIONS	3.00 PM – 3.45 PM	**STANDARD GRADE**
2010		Credit Level
		Reading

Fill in these boxes and read what is printed below.

Full name of centre   Town

Forename(s)   Surname

Date of birth
Day   Month   Year   Scottish candidate number   Number of seat

Do not open this paper until you are told to do so.

When you think you know what to write for each item, write your answer **in English** in the space provided after the item. (You are not expected to fill all the spaces.)

You may use a Gaelic dictionary.

You must write any rough work in this paper.

Before leaving the examination room you must give this book to the Invigilator. If you do not, you may lose all the marks for this paper.

Marks

As part of their course work, students are expected to produce pieces of writing.

1. Alasdair writes about a family holiday in Spain.

An-uiridh, chaidh mi fhèin agus an teaghlach agam air saor-làithean gu taobh an ear na Spàinn agus tha sinn a' dol ann a-rithist airson saor-làithean am-bliadhna. Dh'fhuirich sinn ann an taigh-òsta le amar-snàmh. Bha an taigh-òsta ceart gu leòr ach bha an t-amar-snàmh sgoinneil. Uill, bha trì amaran ann air fad, fear airson pàistean, fear airson clann òga nach eil cho math air snàmh agus amar-snàmh nas motha airson daoine a tha comasach air snàmh. Bha an t-sìde teth agus mar sin chòrd e rium a bhith a' snàmh.

B' e Pàirc-Chleasan Port Aventura a b' fheàrr leam ge-tà. Chaidh sinn ann ceithir tursan agus chaidh sinn gu pàirc-uisge aon turas. Dh'fhuirich sinn aig a' phàirc-chleasan aon oidhche gu meadhan-oidhche airson an taisbeanadh solais fhaicinn. Abair gu robh na solais mìorbhaileach!

(a) When did Alasdair and his family go on holiday to Spain?

_____ 1

(b) Where exactly in Spain did they go?

_____ 1

(c) Where are they going on holiday this year?

_____

_____ 2

Marks

1. **(continued)**

    (*d*) What did Alasdair think of

      (i) the hotel _____ 1

      (ii) the swimming pool? _____ 1

    (*e*) Which swimmers could use the biggest pool?

      _____ 1

    (*f*) Why did he enjoy swimming?

      _____

      _____ 2

    (*g*) What was Alasdair's first comment about the Port Aventura Theme Park?

      _____ 1

    (*h*) Which other park did they visit?

      _____ 1

    (*i*) What happened at midnight in the theme park?

      _____

      _____ 2

[Turn over

Marks

2. Alasdair continues.

Aon latha, chaidh sinn cuairt a dh'fhaicinn Barcelona. Bha neach-iùil air a' bhus ag innse mu eachdraidh an àite. Dh'innis i dhuinn mòran mu na trioblaidean anns an Spàinn aig àm Seanailear Franco. Nuair a ràinig sinn Barcelona thug am bus timcheall a' bhaile sinn agus sheall iad dhuinn àiteachan inntinneach, mar far an robh na Geamannan Oilimpeach nuair a bha iad ann am Barcelona agus cuideachd eaglais nach eil fhathast crìochnaichte. Thadhail sinn cuideachd air an raon-cluiche ball-coise ainmeil "Nou Camp". Bha e ro theth ann am Barcelona anns an Iuchar agus bha mi nam fhallas.

(*a*) What did Alasdair and his family do one day?

_____

_____ 2

(*b*) What was the guide telling them about?

_____

_____ 2

(*c*) What, in particular, did she tell them a lot about?

_____

_____

_____ 3

DO NOT
WRITE IN
THIS
MARGIN

Marks

2. **(continued)**

(*d*) What does he say about a church they saw?

_____

_____ 2

(*e*) What information are we given about the "Nou Camp"?

_____

_____

_____ 3

[Turn over

DO NOT
WRITE IN
THIS
MARGIN

Marks

3. In her article, Rhona writes about having a healthy lifestyle.

Tha e cudromach a bhith fallain. Tha mise a' dèanamh oidhirp mhòr airson a bhith fallain. Airson eacarsaich, bidh mi a' ruith a h-uile dàrna latha agus a' cluich ball-coise nuair as urrainn dhomh. Tha a bhith a' cluich teanas a' còrdadh rium cuideachd. Bidh mi, mar as trice, ag ithe biadh a tha math dhomh. Is toigh leis an teaghlach agam a bhith ag ithe èisg agus glasraich.

Aig an deireadh-sheachdain, ge-tà, is fìor thoigh leam a bhith a' dol do na bùthan agus a bhith a' ceannach seòclaid, suiteis agus 's dòcha brisgein. An uair sin, tha mi ciallach tron t-seachdain a-rithist.

(*a*) What does Rhona say in her first statement?

_____

_____ **2**

(*b*) How often does she go running?

_____

_____

_____ **3**

(*c*) When does she play football?

_____

_____ **2**

DO NOT WRITE IN THIS MARGIN

Marks

3. (continued)

(*d*) What kind of food does her family like to eat?

____

____ **2**

(*e*) When does she buy chocolate and sweets?

____ **1**

(*f*) When is she sensible about what she eats?

____

____ **2**

[Turn over

Marks

4. Callum also writes an article about lifestyle.

Bidh mi a' faighinn tòrr obair-dachaigh. Feumaidh mi a bhith a' dèanamh obair-dachaigh airson dà uair a thìde a h-uile oidhche. Ach, an dèidh na sgoile, airson eacarsaich, thèid mi cuairt leis a' chù chun a' chladaich ri taobh an taighe. 'S e eacarsaich mhath a tha seo dhomh.

Mar as trice, bidh mi ag ithe biadh fallain ach an-dràsta 's a-rithist ithidh mi rudan mar phaidh feòla agus isbeanan. Chan eil iad sin cho math dhomh.

Is lugha orm a bhith a' dol don ionad-spòrs. Tha cus dhaoine ann agus tha e daonnan trang.

(*a*) How long does Callum spend on homework?

_____

_____

_____   3

(*b*) After school, where does Callum go for a walk with his dog? Give a **detailed** answer.

_____

_____

_____   3

DO NOT
WRITE IN
THIS
MARGIN

Marks

4.   **(continued)**

(*c*)   Does Callum consider taking his dog for a walk good exercise?

_____   **1**

(*d*)   What does Callum eat occasionally?

_____

_____   **2**

(*e*)   (i)   Where does Callum hate going?

_____   **1**

(ii)   Why does he hate it?   Give a **detailed** answer.

_____

_____

_____

_____   **4**

[Turn over

Marks

5. Alison writes about a two-day music festival to be held in the town.

Bidh fèis-ciùil anns a' bhaile againn aig deireadh an Iuchair airson dà latha. Chì sibh còmhlain ainmeil agus còmhlain ionadail a bhios sibh eòlach air. Chunnaic sibh na còmhlain ionadail aig consairt "Clann ann an Èis" ann an talla a' bhaile san fhoghar. Rinn an consairt sin £4,000.

Cosgaidh tiogaid fichead 's a còig notaichean airson latha no ceathrad not airson dà latha. Ma tha sibh ag iarraidh, gheibh sibh àite airson campachadh airson deich notaichean. Cuideachd, bidh biadh gu leòr ri fhaighinn aig an fhèis-ciùil.

(*a*) When is the music festival taking place?

_____

_____   2

(*b*) As well as famous bands, who else is performing?

_____   1

(*c*) When was the "Children in Need" concert?

_____   1

(*d*) How much does a two-day ticket cost?

_____   1

(*e*) What can you get at the music festival for £10?

_____

_____   2

Marks

5. (continued)

(*f*) What else is available at the music festival?

_____

_____   2

(60)

[*END OF QUESTION PAPER*]

Page eleven

[BLANK PAGE]

C

1240/406

NATIONAL
QUALIFICATIONS
2010

THURSDAY, 20 MAY
10.30 AM – 11.00 AM

GAELIC (LEARNERS)
STANDARD GRADE
Credit Level
Listening Transcript

This paper must not be seen by any candidate.

The material overleaf is provided for use in an emergency only (eg the recording or equipment proving faulty) or where permission has been given in advance by SQA for the material to be read to candidates with additional support needs. The material must be read exactly as printed.

Transcript—Credit Level

Instructions to reader:

For each item, read the English **once**, and then read the Gaelic **three** times with an interval of seven seconds between the readings. On completion of the third reading, pause for the length of time indicated in brackets after each item, to allow the candidates to write their answers.

The Fourth Year pupils of Glenbeg High School are reading letters from their Canadian pen pals.

Tha sgoilearan na Ceathramh Bliadhna ann an Àrd-sgoil a' Ghlinn Bhig a' leughadh litrichean bho na caraidean-pinn aca à Canada.

Ann has received a letter from Jennifer, one of the Canadian pen pals.

Question number one.

What does Jennifer say at the start of her letter?

> **Dè tha a' dol?**

> (*30 seconds*)

Jennifer talks about school.

Question number two.

(*a*)   Name the subjects she likes in school?

(*b*)   Why does she like one of these subjects?

> **Is toigh leam Beurla agus Cruinn-eòlas anns an sgoil. Is toigh leam Beurla oir tha leughadh a' còrdadh rium.**

> (*30 seconds*)

Jennifer designs clothes in Art, another of the subjects she likes.

Question number three.

(*a*)   What **three** items of clothing does she mention?

> **Bidh mi a' dealbhadh adan, briogaisean agus lèintean.**

> (*40 seconds*)

She also designs skirts.

(*b*)   What do her skirts look like?

> **Tha na sgiortaichean agam fada agus tha flùraichean orra.**

> (*40 seconds*)

Jennifer talks about what she wants to do when she leaves school.

Question number four.

(*a*)   Where does she want to go?

(*b*)   Why does she want to go there?

Bu toigh leam a dhol a Lunnainn oir tha Colaiste Ealain mhath an-sin.

(*40 seconds*)

She continues.

(*c*)   What will she miss when she's away from home?

Bidh mi ag ionndrainn biadh mo mhàthar agus an cat agam nuair a dh'fhalbhas mi.

(*40 seconds*)

Neil reads a letter from Josh, one of the Canadian boys.

Question number five.

What is the weather like where Josh lives? Give a **detailed** answer.

Tha e glè bhlàth anns an t-samhradh.

(*40 seconds*)

Josh goes on to talk about where he lives.

Question number six.

(*a*)   What is it like?

Tha e uabhasach àlainn agus tha mòran sneachd ann.

(*40 seconds*)

He gives more information.

(*b*)   Who comes to the area and why?

Bidh luchd-turais a' tighinn ann airson sgitheadh.

(*30 seconds*)

[Turn over

There are lots of hotels there.

Question number seven.

How much does it cost to stay in the best hotel? Give a **detailed** answer.

Cosgaidh e ceithir cheud dolair gach oidhche anns an taigh-òsta as fheàrr.

(30 seconds)

Josh has a job in this hotel.

Question number eight.

What does he do? Give a **detailed** answer.

'S e còcaire a th' annam agus bidh mi a' dèanamh chèicichean.

(40 seconds)

Josh expresses his opinion about his job.

Question number nine.

(*a*)   What does he say about it?

'S e obair thrang, chruaidh a th' ann.

(30 seconds)

(*b*)   How long has he been doing the job?

Thòisich mi anns an obair seo o chionn bliadhna gu leth.

(30 seconds)

Ann opens the last letter from the Canadians. It is from Melissa, who is a keen ice-skater.

Question number ten.

(*a*)   How old was Melissa when she started skating? Give a **detailed** answer.

(*b*)   In what year did she start?

Bha mi gu bhith ochd bliadhna a dh'aois nuair a thòisich mi ann an dà mhìle 's a h-aon.

(40 seconds)

She explains why she likes ice-skating.

Question number eleven.

Why does Melissa like ice-skating?

> **Is toigh leam a bhith a' spèileadh oir 's e spòrs luath, sgileil a th' ann.**

(30 seconds)

She has been to competitions in other countries.

Question number twelve.

Which **three** countries does she mention?

> **Chaidh mi gu co-fharpaisean ann an Sasainn, anns an Eilbheis agus anns na Stàitean Aonaichte.**

(40 seconds)

She was skating in another town in Canada.

Question number thirteen.

Where, exactly, was this town?

> **'S ann an taobh an iar Chanada a bha e, ceud mìle bho Vancouver.**

(40 seconds)

Ann finishes reading Melissa's letter.

Question number fourteen.

What does Melissa say at the end of her letter?

> **Sgrìobh thugam!**

(30 seconds)

End of test.

Now look over your answers.

[END OF TRANSCRIPT]

[BLANK PAGE]

C

FOR OFFICIAL USE

Total
Mark

1240/405

NATIONAL
QUALIFICATIONS
2010

THURSDAY, 20 MAY
10.30 AM – 11.00 AM

GAELIC (LEARNERS)
STANDARD GRADE
Credit Level
Listening

Fill in these boxes and read what is printed below.

Full name of centre

Town

Forename(s)

Surname

Date of birth
Day   Month   Year   Scottish candidate number   Number of seat

Do not open this paper until you are told to do so.

In this test, you have to listen carefully to a number of short passages in Gaelic to find the information asked for in the questions.

You will hear each passage three times, and then you will have time to write your answers. Answer **in English** in the spaces provided.

When you are told to open this paper, read the English introduction at the beginning. Follow the questions printed in the paper as you hear them, and then write your answers. Do not give up the first time you get stuck; leave a blank and keep trying.

As you listen to the passages, you may make notes, but only in this paper.

You are not allowed to leave the examination room until the end of the test.

Before leaving the examination room you must give this book to the Invigilator. If you do not, you may lose all the marks for this paper.

Marks

The Fourth Year pupils of Glenbeg High School are reading letters from their Canadian pen pals.

Ann has received a letter from Jennifer, one of the Canadian pen pals.

1. What does Jennifer say at the start of her letter?

_____

_____ 2

*   *   *   *   *

Jennifer talks about school.

2. (*a*) Name the subjects she likes in school.

_____

_____ 2

(*b*) Why does she like one of these subjects?

_____

_____ 2

*   *   *   *   *

Jennifer designs clothes in Art, another of the subjects she likes.

3. (*a*) What **three** items of clothing does she mention?

_____

_____

_____ 3

She also designs skirts.

(*b*) What do her skirts look like?

_____

_____ 2

*   *   *   *   *

Marks

Jennifer talks about what she wants to do when she leaves school.

4. (*a*) Where does she want to go?

_____   **1**

(*b*) Why does she want to go there?

_____

_____

_____   **3**

She continues.

(*c*) What will she miss when she's away from home?

_____

_____

_____   **3**

*   *   *   *   *

Neil reads a letter from Josh, one of the Canadian boys.

5. What is the weather like where Josh lives? Give a **detailed** answer.

_____

_____

_____   **3**

*   *   *   *   *

[Turn over

Josh goes on to talk about where he lives.

6. (*a*) What is it like?

_____

_____

_____

_____   **4**

He gives more information.

(*b*) Who comes to the area and why?

_____

_____   **2**

*   *   *   *   *

There are lots of hotels there.

7. How much does it cost to stay in the best hotel? Give a **detailed** answer.

_____

_____   **2**

*   *   *   *   *

Marks

Josh has a job in this hotel.

8. What does he do? Give a **detailed** answer.

_____

_____

_____   3

*   *   *   *   *

Josh expresses his opinion about his job.

9. (*a*) What does he say about it?

_____

_____   2

(*b*) How long has he been doing the job?

_____

_____   2

*   *   *   *   *

[Turn over

Marks

Ann opens the last letter from the Canadians. It is from Melissa, who is a keen ice-skater.

10. (*a*) How old was Melissa when she started skating? Give a **detailed** answer.

_____

_____ 2

(*b*) In what year did she start?

_____ 1

* * * *

She explains why she likes ice-skating.

11. Why does Melissa like ice-skating?

_____

_____ 2

* * * * *

Marks

She has been to competitions in other countries.

12. Which **three** countries does she mention?

_____

_____

_____ 3

* * * * *

She was skating in another town in Canada.

13. Where, exactly, was this town?

_____

_____

_____

_____ 4

* * * * *

Ann finishes reading Melissa's letter.

14. What does Melissa say at the end of her letter?

_____

_____ 2

* * * * *

Total marks (50)

[END OF QUESTION PAPER]

[BLANK PAGE]

[BLANK PAGE]

G
C

1241/410

NATIONAL
QUALIFICATIONS
2010

THURSDAY, 20 MAY
11.15 AM – 12.15 PM

GAELIC (LEARNERS)
STANDARD GRADE
General/Credit Level
(Optional)
Writing

Do not turn over this paper until you are told to do so.

You may use a Gaelic dictionary.

Write your answer in the booklet provided.

Choose ONE question from the following four questions.

Write your answer, in Gaelic, in the answer booklet provided.

You must answer in sentences. To help you write, you have been given checklists, graphics and a suggested way to start each piece.

EITHER

1.   You are writing a blog about a concert, or other event, that you have been at.

     You **may** include the following points:

- what the event was
- where it was held
- when it was held
- how much it cost
- who went with you
- when it started/finished
- whether you enjoyed it and why
- any other information.

Bha mi aig consairt . . .

OR

2.   You have been on holiday and are writing about it for the school magazine.

You **may** include the following points:

*   where you went

*   how you got there

*   where you were staying

*   what you did

*   what the weather was like

*   what you bought

*   whether you enjoyed it and why

*   any other information.

Làithean-saora

Chaidh sinn gu . . .

[Turn over

OR

3. You have been on a school trip and you have been asked to write about it in your Gaelic class.

    You **may** include the following points:

    •   where you went

    •   how long you went for

    •   who went with you

    •   what the trip was for

    •   what you did

    •   what the weather was like

    •   whether you enjoyed it and why

    •   any other information.

Turas-sgoile

Diluain: Tha an turas seo . . .

OR

4.   You have been asked to write a profile of yourself to send to a penpal.

You **may** include the following points:

- your name
- your age
- what you look like
- your likes and dislikes
- your hobbies
- your family
- what subjects you do in school
- any other information.

Mise

Is mise Màiri agus . . .

[END OF QUESTION PAPER]

[BLANK PAGE]

[BLANK PAGE]

[BLANK PAGE]